The Poetry of James Thomson

Volume I (of III) - The Seasons

James Thomson was born in Ednam in Roxburghshire around 11th September 1700 and baptised on 15th September. He was the fourth of nine children to father Thomas, the Presbyterian minister of Ednam and mother Beatrix.

Apart from the exact date of his birth several other facts of his life cannot be verified.

It is thought Thomson may have attended the parish school of Southdean, his father having been appointed minster there a few months after the birth of his son, before attending the grammar school in Jedburgh in 1712. Accounts of his early abilities are almost always negative. Poetry however was his great love. In this he was encouraged by Robert Riccaltoun, a farmer, poet and Presbyterian minister; and Sir William Bennet, a whig laird who was also the patron of Allan Ramsay. Very few early poems by Thomson survive. It seems that on each New Year's Day he burned almost all of his year's output.

In the autumn of 1715 he entered the College of Edinburgh on a career path that would take him to the Presbyterian ministry. In college he studied metaphysics, Logic, Ethics, Greek, Latin and Natural Philosophy. He also became a member of the Grotesque Club, a literary group. Here he met his lifelong friend to be; David Mallet.

In 1716 his father, Thomas, died. Again, facts are hard to come by but there is a colourful local legend that he died whilst performing an exorcism.

In 1719 Thomson completed his arts course but rather than graduate he instead entered Divinity Hall to become a minister.

However Thomson was also keen on literary pursuits. He managed to obtain publication of several of his poems in the 'Edinburgh Miscellany'. With this as his calling card he followed Mallet to London in February 1725 in an attempt at further publishing success. For Thomson a career as a minister was now behind him.

In London, Thomson became a tutor to the son of Charles Hamilton, Lord Binning, via connections on his mother's side of the family. Through David Mallet, who by 1724 was now also a published poet, Thomson met the great English poets of the day including Richard Savage, Aaron Hill and Alexander Pope.

Beatrix, Thomson's mother died on 12th May 1725, around the time of his writing 'Winter', the first poem of 'The Seasons'. 'Winter' was first published by John Millian in 1726 with a second edition incorporating revisions, additions and a preface later that same year.

By 1727, Thomson was working on 'Summer', which he published in February, whilst working at Watt's Academy, a school for young gentlemen and a centre of Newtonian science.

That same year Millian published Thomson's 'A Poem to the Memory of Sir Isaac Newton' in memory of the great scientist who had passed in March.

Thomson now left Watt's academy hoping to further pursue his career. This was greatly helped by finding several patrons including Thomas Rundle, the countess of Hertford and Charles Talbot, 1st Baron Talbot.

Thomson worked hard to complete 'The Seasons' during the late 1720's. 'Spring' was completed in 1728 and finally Autumn in 1730. Now the complete set of four could be published together as 'The Seasons'.

During this period he also wrote other poems, as well as a play, his first, 'The Tragedy of Sophonisba' in 1729. The latter is best known today for its mention in Samuel Johnson's Lives of the English Poets, where Johnson records that one 'feeble' line of the poem – "O, Sophonisba, Sophonisba, O!" was parodied by the wags of the theatre as, "O, Jemmy Thomson, Jemmy Thomson, O!"

In 1730, he was appointed tutor to the son of Sir Charles Talbot, his patron and also Solicitor-General. Thomson would spend nearly two years with the young man on 'the grand tour' of Europe. On his return Talbot graciously arranged for Thomson to become a secretary in chancery, which gave him financial security during until Talbot's death in 1737. Meanwhile, in 1734 Thomson's major work 'Liberty' was published.

In 1740, he collaborated with Mallet on the masque 'Alfred' which was first performed at Cliveden, the country home of Frederick, Prince of Wales. Thomson's words for 'Rule Britannia', from that masque, and set to music by Thomas Arne, became one of the best-known British patriotic songs. The Prince settled on him a pension of £100 per annum. He also introduced him to George Lyttelton, who became his friend and patron.

In later years, Thomson lived in Richmond upon Thames, and it was there that he wrote his final work 'The Castle of Indolence', which was published just before his untimely death on 27th August 1748. Johnson writes on Thomson's death that "by taking cold on the water between London and Kew, he caught a disorder, which, with some careless exasperation, ended in a fever that put end to his life".

He was buried in St. Mary Magdalene church in Richmond.

Index of Contents
THE SEASONS
Spring
Summer
Autumn
Winter
WINTER: A PREFACE (for the second edition)
A HYMN ON THE SEASONS
A CHRONOLOGY TO ELUCIDATE AND ILLUSTRATE THELIFE AND TIMES OF JAMES THOMSON

THE SEASONS: A POEM

SPRING

The Argument

The subject proposed. Inscribed to the Countess of Hartford. The Season is described as it affects the various parts of nature, ascending from the lower to the higher; and mixed with digressions arising from the subject. Its influence on inanimate matter, on vegetables, on brute animals, and last on Man; concluding with a dissuasive from the wild and irregular passion of Love, opposed to that of a pure and happy kind.

Come, gentle Spring, ethereal mildness, come;
And from the bosom of yon dropping cloud,
While music wakes around, veiled in a shower
Of shadowing roses, on our plains descend.

O Hartford, fitted or to shine in courts
With unaffected grace, or walk the plain
With innocence and meditation joined
In soft assemblage, listen to my song,
Which thy own season paints—when nature all
Is blooming and benevolent, like thee.

And see where surly Winter passes off
Far to the north, and calls his ruffian blasts:
His blasts obey, and quit the howling hill,
The shattered forest, and the ravaged vale;
While softer gales succeed, at whose kind touch,
Dissolving snows in livid torrents lost,
The mountains lift their green heads to the sky.

As yet the trembling year is unconfirmed,
And Winter oft at eve resumes the breeze,
Chills the pale morn, and bids his driving sleets
Deform the day delightless; so that scarce
The bittern knows his time with bill engulfed
To shake the sounding marsh; or from the shore
The plovers when to scatter o'er the heath,
And sing their wild notes to the listening waste.

At last from Aries rolls the bounteous sun,
And the bright Bull receives him. Then no more
The expansive atmosphere is cramped with cold;
But, full of life and vivifying soul,
Lifts the light clouds sublime, and spreads them thin,
Fleecy, and white o'er all-surrounding heaven.

Forth fly the tepid airs; and unconfined,
Unbinding earth, the moving softness strays.
Joyous the impatient husbandman perceives
Relenting Nature, and his lusty steers
Drives from their stalls to where the well-used plough
Lies in the furrow loosened from the frost.
There, unrefusing, to the harnessed yoke
They lend their shoulder, and begin their toil,
Cheered by the simple song and soaring lark.
Meanwhile incumbent o'er the shining share
The master leans, removes the obstructing clay,
Winds the whole work, and sidelong lays the glebe.

White through the neighbouring fields the sower stalks
With measured step, and liberal throws the grain
Into the faithful bosom of the ground:
The harrow follows harsh, and shuts the scene.

Be gracious, Heaven, for now laborious man
Has done his part. Ye fostering breezes, blow;
Ye softening dews, ye tender showers, descend;
And temper all, thou world-reviving sun,
Into the perfect year. Nor, ye who live
In luxury and ease, in pomp and pride,
Think these lost themes unworthy of your ear:
Such themes as these the rural Maro sung
To wide-imperial Rome, in the full height
Of elegance and taste, by Greece refined.
In ancient times the sacred plough employed
The kings and awful fathers of mankind;
And some, with whom compared your insect-tribes
Are but the beings of a summer's day,
Have held the scale of empire, ruled the storm
Of mighty war; then, with victorious hand,
Disdaining little delicacies, seized
The plough, and greatly independent scorned
All the vile stores corruption can bestow.

Ye generous Britons, venerate the plough;
And o'er your hills and long withdrawing vales
Let Autumn spread his treasures to the sun,
Luxuriant and unbounded. As the sea
Far through his azure turbulent domain
Your empire owns, and from a thousand shores
Wafts all the pomp of life into your ports;
So with superior boon may your rich soil,
Exuberant, Nature's better blessings pour

O'er every land, the naked nations clothe,
And be the exhaustless granary of a world!

Nor only through the lenient air this change
Delicious breathes: the penetrative sun,
His force deep-darting to the dark retreat
Of vegetation, sets the steaming power
At large, to wander o'er the vernant earth
In various hues; but chiefly thee, gay green!
Thou smiling Nature's universal robe!
United light and shade! where the sight dwells
With growing strength and ever-new delight.

From the moist meadow to the withered hill,
Led by the breeze, the vivid verdure runs,
And swells and deepens to the cherished eye.
The hawthorn whitens; and the juicy groves
Put forth their buds, unfolding by degrees,
Till the whole leafy forest stands display'd
In full luxuriance to the sighing gales—
Where the deer rustle through the twining brake,
And the birds sing concealed. At once arrayed
In all the colours of the flushing year
By Nature's swift and secret-working hand,
The garden glows, and fills the liberal air
With lavish fragrance; while the promised fruit
Lies yet a little embryo, unperceived,
Within its crimson folds. Now from the town,
Buried in smoke and sleep and noisome damps,
Oft let me wander o'er the dewy fields
Where freshness breathes, and dash the trembling drops
From the bent bush, as through the verdant maze
Of sweet-briar hedges I pursue my walk;
Or taste the smell of dairy; or ascend
Some eminence, Augusta, in thy plains,
And see the country, far-diffused around,
One boundless blush, one white-empurpled shower
Of mingled blossoms; where the raptured eye
Hurries from joy to joy, and, hid beneath
The fair profusion, yellow Autumn spies.

If, brushed from Russian wilds, a cutting gale
Rise not, and scatter from his humid wings
The clammy mildew; or, dry-blowing, breathe
Untimely frost—before whose baleful blast
The full-blown Spring through all her foliage shrinks,
Joyless and dead, a wide-dejected waste.
For oft, engendered by the hazy north,

Myriads on myriads, insect armies waft
Keen in the poisoned breeze, and wasteful eat
Through buds and bark into the blackened core
Their eager way. A feeble race, yet oft
The sacred sons of vengeance, on whose course
Corrosive famine waits, and kills the year.
To check this plague, the skilful farmer chaff
And blazing straw before his orchard burns;
Till, all involved in smoke, the latent foe
From every cranny suffocated falls;
Or scatters o'er the blooms the pungent dust
Of pepper, fatal to the frosty tribe;
Or, when the envenomed leaf begins to curl,
With sprinkled water drowns them in their nest:
Nor, while they pick them up with busy bill,
The little trooping birds unwisely scares.

Be patient, swains; these cruel-seeming winds
Blow not in vain. Far hence they keep repressed
Those deepening clouds on clouds, surcharged with rain,
That o'er the vast Atlantic hither borne
In endless train would quench the Summer blaze,
And cheerless drown the crude unripened year.

The North-east spends his rage, and, now shut up
Within his iron caves, the effusive South
Warms the wide air, and o'er the void of heaven
Breathes the big clouds with vernal showers distent.
At first a dusky wreath they seem to rise,
Scarce staining ether; but by fast degrees,
In heaps on heaps the doubling vapour sails
Along the loaded sky, and mingling deep
Sits on the horizon round a settled gloom;
Not such as wintry storms on mortals shed,
Oppressing life; but lovely, gentle, kind,
And full of every hope and every joy,
The wish of Nature. Gradual sinks the breeze
Into a perfect calm; that not a breath
Is heard to quiver through the closing woods,
Or rustling turn the many-twinkling leaves
Of aspen tall. The uncurling floods, diffused
In glassy breadth, seem through delusive lapse
Forgetful of their course. 'Tis silence all,
And pleasing expectation. Herds and flocks
Drop the dry sprig, and mute-imploring eye
The falling verdure. Hushed in short suspense,
The plumy people streak their wings with oil
To throw the lucid moisture trickling off,

And wait the approaching sign to strike at once
Into the general choir. Even mountains, vales,
And forests seem, impatient, to demand
The promised sweetness. Man superior walks
Amid the glad creation, musing praise
And looking lively gratitude. At last
The clouds consign their treasures to the fields,
And, softly shaking on the dimpled pool
Prelusive drops, let all their moisture flow
In large effusion o'er the freshened world.
The stealing shower is scarce to patter heard
By such as wander through the forest-walks,
Beneath the umbrageous multitude of leaves:
But who can hold the shade while Heaven descends
In universal bounty, shedding herbs
And fruits and flowers on Nature's ample lap?
Swift fancy fired anticipates their growth;
And, while the milky nutriment distils,
Beholds the kindling country colour round.

Thus all day long the full-distended clouds
Indulge their genial stores, and well-showered earth
Is deep enriched with vegetable life;
Till, in the western sky, the downward sun
Looks out effulgent from amid the flush
Of broken clouds, gay-shifting to his beam.
The rapid radiance instantaneous strikes
The illumined mountain, through the forest streams,
Shakes on the floods, and in a yellow mist,
Far smoking o'er the interminable plain,
In twinkling myriads lights the dewy gems.
Moist, bright, and green, the landscape laughs around.
Full swell the woods; their every music wakes,
Mixed in wild concert, with the warbling brooks
Increased, the distant bleatings of the hills,
The hollow lows responsive from the vales,
Whence, blending all, the sweetened zephyr springs.
Meantime, refracted from yon eastern cloud,
Bestriding earth, the grand ethereal bow
Shoots up immense; and every hue unfolds,
From the white mingling maze. Not so the swain;
He wondering views the bright enchantment bend
Delightful o'er the radiant fields, and runs
To catch the falling glory; but amazed
Beholds the amusive arch before him fly,
Then vanish quite away. Still night succeeds,
A softened shade, and saturated earth
Awaits the morning beam, to give to light,

Raised through ten thousand different plastic tubes,
The balmy treasures of the former day.

Then spring the living herbs, profusely wild,
O'er all the deep-green earth, beyond the power
Of botanist to number up their tribes:
Whether he steals along the lonely dale
In silent search; or through the forest, rank
With what the dull incurious weeds account,
Bursts his blind way; or climbs the mountain-rock,
Fired by the nodding verdure of its brow.
With such a liberal hand has Nature flung
Their seeds abroad, blown them about in winds,
Innumerous mixed them with the nursing mould,
The moistening current, and prolific rain.

But who their virtues can declare? who pierce
With vision pure into these secret stores
Of health and life and joy? the food of man
While yet he lived in innocence, and told
A length of golden years, unfleshed in blood,
A stranger to the savage arts of life,
Death, rapine, carnage, surfeit, and disease—
The lord and not the tyrant of the world.

The first fresh dawn then waked the gladdened race
Of uncorrupted man, nor blushed to see
The sluggard sleep beneath its sacred beam;
For their light slumbers gently fumed away,
And up they rose as vigorous as the sun,
Or to the culture of the willing glebe,
Or to the cheerful tendance of the flock.
Meantime the song went round; and dance and sport,
Wisdom and friendly talk successive stole
Their hours away; while in the rosy vale
Love breathed his infant sighs, from anguish free,
And full replete with bliss—save the sweet pain
That, inly thrilling, but exalts it more.
Nor yet injurious act nor surly deed
Was known among these happy sons of heaven;
For reason and benevolence were law.
Harmonious Nature too looked smiling on.
Clear shone the skies, cooled with eternal gales,
And balmy spirit all. The youthful sun
Shot his best rays, and still the gracious clouds
Dropped fatness down; as o'er the swelling mead
The herds and flocks commixing played secure.
This when, emergent from the gloomy wood,

The glaring lion saw, his horrid heart
Was meekened, and he joined his sullen joy.
For music held the whole in perfect peace:
Soft sighed the flute; the tender voice was heard,
Warbling the varied heart; the woodlands round
Applied their quire; and winds and waters flowed
In consonance. Such were those prime of days.

But now those white unblemished minutes, whence,
The fabling poets took their golden age,
Are found no more amid these iron times,
These dregs of life! Now the distempered mind
Has lost that concord of harmonious powers
Which forms the soul of happiness; and all
Is off the poise within: the passions all
Have burst their bounds; and Reason, half extinct,
Or impotent, or else approving, sees
The foul disorder. Senseless and deformed,
Convulsive Anger storms at large; or, pale
And silent, settles into fell revenge.
Base Envy withers at another's joy,
And hates that excellence it cannot reach.
Desponding Fear, of feeble fancies full,
Weak and unmanly, loosens every power.
Even Love itself is bitterness of soul,
A pensive anguish pining at the heart;
Or, sunk to sordid interest, feels no more
That noble wish, that never-cloyed desire,
Which, selfish joy disdaining, seeks alone
To bless the dearer object of its flame.
Hope sickens with extravagance; and Grief,
Of life impatient, into madness swells,
Or in dead silence wastes the weeping hours.
These, and a thousand mixt emotions more,
From ever-changing views of good and ill,
Formed infinitely various, vex the mind
With endless storm: whence, deeply rankling, grows
The partial thought, a listless unconcern,
Cold, and averting from our neighbour's good;
Then dark disgust and hatred, winding wiles,
Coward deceit, and ruffian violence.
At last, extinct each social feeling, fell
And joyless inhumanity pervades
And petrifies the heart. Nature disturbed
Is deemed, vindictive, to have changed her course.

Hence, in old dusky time, a deluge came:
When the deep-cleft disparting orb, that arched

The central waters round, impetuous rushed
With universal burst into the gulf,
And o'er the high-piled hills of fractured earth
Wide-dashed the waves in undulation vast,
Till, from the centre to the streaming clouds,
A shoreless ocean tumbled round the globe.

The Seasons since have, with severer sway,
Oppressed a broken world: the Winter keen
Shook forth his waste of snows; and Summer shot
His pestilential heats. Great Spring before
Greened all the year; and fruits and blossoms blushed
In social sweetness on the self-same bough.
Pure was the temperate air; an even calm
Perpetual reigned, save what the zephyrs bland
Breathed o'er the blue expanse: for then nor storms
Were taught to blow, nor hurricanes to rage;
Sound slept the waters; no sulphureous glooms
Swelled in the sky and sent the lightning forth;
While sickly damps and cold autumnal fogs
Hung not relaxing on the springs of life.
But now, of turbid elements the sport,
From clear to cloudy tossed, from hot to cold,
And dry to moist, with inward-eating change,
Our drooping days are dwindled down to naught,
Their period finished ere 'tis well begun.

And yet the wholesome herb neglected dies;

Though with the pure exhilarating soul
Of nutriment and health, and vital powers,
Beyond the search of art, 'tis copious blest.
For, with hot ravine fired, ensanguined man
Is now become the lion of the plain, And worse.
The wolf, who from the nightly fold
Fierce drags the bleating prey, ne'er drunk her milk,
Nor wore her warming fleece: nor has the steer,
At whose strong chest the deadly tiger hangs,
E'er ploughed for him. They too are tempered high,
With hunger stung and wild necessity,
Nor lodges pity in their shaggy breast.
But man, whom Nature formed of milder clay,
With every kind emotion in his heart,
And taught alone to weep,—while from her lap
She pours ten thousand delicacies, herbs
And fruits, as numerous as the drops of rain
Or beams that gave them birth,—shall he, fair form!
Who wears sweet smiles, and looks erect on Heaven,

E'er stoop to mingle with the prowling herd,
And dip his tongue in gore? The beast of prey,
Blood-stained, deserves to bleed: but you, ye flocks,
What have ye done? ye peaceful people, what,
To merit death? you, who have given us milk
In luscious streams, and lent us your own coat
Against the Winter's cold? And the plain ox,
That harmless, honest, guileless animal,
In what has he offended? he, whose toil,
Patient and ever ready, clothes the land
With all the pomp of harvest; shall he bleed,
And struggling groan beneath the cruel hands
Even of the clowns he feeds? And that, perhaps,
To swell the riot of the autumnal feast,
Won by his labour? This the feeling heart
Would tenderly suggest: but 'tis enough,
In this late age, adventurous to have touched
Light on the numbers of the Samian Sage.
High Heaven forbids the bold presumptuous strain,
Whose wisest will has fixed us in a state
That must not yet to pure perfection rise:
Besides, who knows, how, raised to higher life,
From stage to stage, the vital scale ascends?

Now, when the first foul torrent of the brooks,
Swelled with the vernal rains, is ebbed away,
And whitening down their mossy-tinctured stream
Descends the billowy foam; now is the time,
While yet the dark-brown water aids the guile,
To tempt the trout. The well-dissembled fly,
The rod fine-tapering with elastic spring,
Snatched from the hoary steed the floating line,
And all thy slender watery stores prepare.
But let not on thy hook the tortured worm
Convulsive twist in agonizing folds;
Which, by rapacious hunger swallowed deep,
Gives, as you tear it from the bleeding breast
Of the weak helpless uncomplaining wretch,
Harsh pain and horror to the tender hand.

When with his lively ray the potent sun
Has pierced the streams and roused the finny race,
Then, issuing cheerful, to thy sport repair;
Chief should the western breezes curling play,
And light o'er ether bear the shadowy clouds.
High to their fount, this day, amid the hills
And woodlands warbling round, trace up the brooks;
The next, pursue their rocky-channelled maze,

Down to the river, in whose ample wave
Their little naiads love to sport at large.
Just in the dubious point where with the pool
Is mixed the trembling stream, or where it boils
Around the stone, or from the hollowed bank
Reverted plays in undulating flow,
There throw, nice-judging, the delusive fly;
And, as you lead it round in artful curve,
With eye attentive mark the springing game.
Straight as above the surface of the flood
The speckled infant throw. But, should you lure
From his dark haunt beneath the tangled roots
Of pendent trees the monarch of the brook,
Behoves you then to ply your finest art.
Long time he, following cautious, scans the fly,
And oft attempts to seize it, but as oft
The dimpled water speaks his jealous fear.
At last, while haply o'er the shaded sun
Passes a cloud, he desperate takes the death
With sullen plunge. At once he darts along,
Deep-struck, and runs out all the lengthened line;
Then seeks the farthest ooze, the sheltering weed,
The caverned bank, his old secure abode;
And flies aloft, and flounces round the pool,
Indignant of the guile. With yielding hand,
That feels him still, yet to his furious course
Gives way, you, now retiring, following now
Across the stream, exhaust his idle rage;
Till floating broad upon his breathless side,
And to his fate abandoned, to the shore
You gaily drag your unresisting prize.

Thus pass the temperate hours: but when the sun
Shakes from his noon-day throne the scattering clouds,
Even shooting listless languor through the deeps,
Then seek the bank where flowering elders crowd,
Where scattered wild the lily of the vale
Its balmy essence breathes, where cowslips hang
The dewy head, where purple violets lurk,
With all the lowly children of the shade;
Or lie reclined beneath yon spreading ash
Hung o'er the steep, whence, borne on liquid wing,

The sounding culver shoots, or where the hawk,
High in the beetling cliff, his eyry builds.
There let the classic page thy fancy lead
Through rural scenes, such as the Mantuan swain
Paints in the matchless harmony of song;

Or catch thyself the landscape, gliding swift
Athwart imagination's vivid eye;
Or, by the vocal woods and waters lulled,
And lost in lonely musing, in a dream
Confused of careless solitude where mix
Ten thousand wandering images of things,
Soothe every gust of passion into peace—
All but the swellings of the softened heart,
That waken, not disturb, the tranquil mind.

Behold yon breathing prospect bids the Muse
Throw all her beauty forth. But who can paint
Like Nature? Can imagination boast,
Amid its gay creation, hues like hers?
Or can it mix them with that matchless skill,
And lose them in each other, as appears
In every bud that blows? If fancy then
Unequal fails beneath the pleasing task,
Ah, what shall language do? ah, where find words
Tinged with so many colours and whose power,
To life approaching, may perfume my lays
With that fine oil, those aromatic gales
That inexhaustive flow continual round?

Yet, though successless, will the toil delight.
Come then, ye virgins and ye youths, whose hearts
Have felt the raptures of refining love;
And thou, Amanda, come, pride of my song!
Formed by the Graces, loveliness itself!
Come with those downcast eyes, sedate and sweet,
Those looks demure that deeply pierce the soul,
Where, with the light of thoughtful reason mixed,
Shines lively fancy and the feeling heart:
Oh, come! and, while the rosy-footed May
Steals blushing on, together let us tread
The morning dews, and gather in their prime
Fresh-blooming flowers to grace thy braided hair
And thy loved bosom, that improves their sweets.

See where the winding vale its lavish stores,
Irriguous, spreads. See how the lily drinks
The latent rill, scarce oozing through the grass
Of growth luxuriant, or the humid bank
In fair profusion decks. Long let us walk
Where the breeze blows from yon extended field
Of blossomed beans. Arabia cannot boast
A fuller gale of joy than liberal thence
Breathes through the sense, and takes the ravished soul.

Nor is the mead unworthy of thy foot,
Full of fresh verdure and unnumbered flowers,
The negligence of nature wide and wild,
Where, undisguised by mimic art, she spreads
Unbounded beauty to the roving eye.
Here their delicious task the fervent bees
In swarming millions tend. Around, athwart,
Through the soft air, the busy nations fly,
Cling to the bud, and with inserted tube
Suck its pure essence, its ethereal soul.
And oft with bolder wing they soaring dare
The purple heath, or where the wild thyme grows,
And yellow load them with the luscious spoil.

At length the finished garden to the view
Its vistas opens and its alleys green.
Snatched through the verdant maze, the hurried eye
Distracted wanders; now the bowery walk
Of covert close, where scarce a speck of day
Falls on the lengthened gloom, protracted sweeps;
Now meets the bending sky, the river now
Dimpling along, the breezy ruffled lake,
The forest darkening round, the glittering spire,
The ethereal mountain, and the distant main.
But why so far excursive? when at hand,
Along these blushing borders bright with dew,
And in yon mingled wilderness of flowers,
Fair-handed Spring unbosoms every grace—
Throws out the snow-drop and the crocus first,
The daisy, primrose, violet darkly blue,
And polyanthus of unnumbered dyes;
The yellow wall-flower, stained with iron brown,
And lavish stock, that scents the garden round:
From the soft wing of vernal breezes shed,
Anemones; auriculas, enriched
With shining meal o'er all their velvet leaves;
And full ranunculus of glowing red.
Then comes the tulip-race, where beauty plays
Her idle freaks: from family diffused
To family, as flies the father-dust,
The varied colours run; and, while they break
On the charmed eye, the exulting florist marks
With secret pride the wonders of his hand.

No gradual bloom is wanting-from the bud
First-born of Spring to Summer's musky tribes;
Nor hyacinths, of purest virgin white,
Low bent and blushing inward; nor jonquils,

Of potent fragrance; nor narcissus fair,
As o'er the fabled fountain hanging still;
Nor broad carnations, nor gay-spotted pinks;
Nor, showered from every bush, the damask-rose:
Infinite numbers, delicacies, smells,
With hues on hues expression cannot paint,
The breath of Nature, and her endless bloom.

Hail, Source of Being! Universal Soul
Of heaven and earth! Essential Presence, hail!
To thee I bend the knee; to thee my thoughts
Continual climb, who with a master-hand
Hast the great whole into perfection touched.
By thee the various vegetative tribes,
Wrapt in a filmy net and clad with leaves,
Draw the live ether and imbibe the dew.
By thee disposed into congenial soils,
Stands each attractive plant, and sucks, and swells
The juicy tide, a twining mass of tubes.
At thy command the vernal sun awakes
The torpid sap, detruded to the root
By wintry winds, that now in fluent dance
And lively fermentation mounting spreads
All this innumerous-coloured scene of things.
My theme ascends, with equal wing ascend,
My panting muse; and hark, how loud the woods

Invite you forth in all your gayest trim.
Lend me your song, ye nightingales! oh, pour
The mazy-running soul of melody
Into my varied verse! while I deduce,
From the first note the hollow cuckoo sings,
The symphony of Spring, and touch a theme
Unknown to fame-the passion of the groves.

When first the soul of love is sent abroad
Warm through the vital air, and on the heart
Harmonious seizes, the gay troops begin
In gallant thought to plume the painted wing;
And try again the long-forgotten strain,
At first faint-warbled. But no sooner grows
The soft infusion prevalent and wide
Than all alive at once their joy o'erflows
In music unconfined. Up springs the lark,
Shrill-voiced and loud, the messenger of morn:
Ere yet the shadows fly, he mounted sings
Amid the dawning clouds, and from their haunts
Calls up the tuneful nations. Every copse

Deep-tangled, tree irregular, and bush
Bending with dewy moisture o'er the heads
Of the coy quiristers that lodge within,
Are prodigal of harmony. The thrush
And wood-lark, o'er the kind-contending throng
Superior heard, run through the sweetest length
Of notes, when listening Philomela deigns
To let them joy, and purposes, in thought
Elate, to make her night excel their day.
The blackbird whistles from the thorny brake,
The mellow bullfinch answers from the grove;
Nor are the linnets, o'er the flowering furze
Poured out profusely, silent. Joined to these
Innumerous songsters, in the freshening shade
Of new-sprung leaves, their modulations mix
Mellifluous. The jay, the rook, the daw,
And each harsh pipe, discordant heard alone,
Aid the full concert; while the stock-dove breathes
A melancholy murmur through the whole.

'Tis love creates their melody, and all
This waste of music is the voice of love,
That even to birds and beasts the tender arts
Of pleasing teaches. Hence the glossy kind
Try every winning way inventive love
Can dictate, and in courtship to their mates
Pour forth their little souls. First, wide around,
With distant awe, in airy rings they rove,
Endeavouring by a thousand tricks to catch
The cunning, conscious, half-averted glance
Of their regardless charmer. Should she seem
Softening the least approvance to bestow,
Their colours burnish, and, by hope inspired,
They brisk advance; then, on a sudden struck,
Retire disordered; then again approach,
In fond rotation spread the spotted wing,
And shiver every feather with desire.

Connubial leagues agreed, to the deep woods
They haste away, all as their fancy leads,
Pleasure, or food, or secret safety prompts;
That Nature's great command may be obeyed,
Nor all the sweet sensations they perceive
Indulged in vain. Some to the holly-hedge
Nestling repair, and to the thicket some;
Some to the rude protection of the thorn
Commit their feeble offspring. The cleft tree
Offers its kind concealment to a few,

Their food its insects, and its moss their nests.
Others apart far in the grassy dale,
Or roughening waste, their humble texture weave
But most in woodland solitudes delight,
In unfrequented glooms, or shaggy banks,
Steep, and divided by a babbling brook
Whose murmurs soothe them all the live-long day
When by kind duty fixed. Among the roots
Of hazel, pendent o'er the plaintive stream,
They frame the first foundation of their domes—
Dry sprigs of trees, in artful fabric laid,
And bound with clay together. Now 'tis nought
But restless hurry through the busy air,
Beat by unnumbered wings. The swallow sweeps
The slimy pool, to build his hanging house
Intent. And often, from the careless back
Of herds and flocks, a thousand tugging bills
Pluck hair and wool; and oft, when unobserved,
Steal from the barn a straw-till soft and warm,
Clean and complete, their habitation grows.

As thus the patient dam assiduous sits,
Not to be tempted from her tender task
Or by sharp hunger or by smooth delight,
Though the whole loosened Spring around her blows,
Her sympathizing lover takes his stand
High on the opponent bank, and ceaseless sings
The tedious time away; or else supplies
Her place a moment, while she sudden flits
To pick the scanty meal. The appointed time
With pious toil fulfilled, the callow young,
Warmed and expanded into perfect life,
Their brittle bondage break, and come to light,
A helpless family demanding food
With constant clamour. Oh, what passions then,
What melting sentiments of kindly care,
On the new parents seize! Away they fly
Affectionate, and undesiring bear
The most delicious morsel to their young;
Which equally distributed, again
The search begins. Even so a gentle pair,
By fortune sunk, but formed of generous mould,
And charmed with cares beyond the vulgar breast,
In some lone cot amid the distant woods,
Sustain'd alone by providential Heaven,
Oft, as they weeping eye their infant train,
Check their own appetites, and give them all.

Nor toil alone they scorn: exalting love,
By the great Father of the Spring inspired,
Gives instant courage to the fearful race,
And to the simple art. With stealthy wing,
Should some rude foot their woody haunts molest,
Amid a neighbouring bush they silent drop,
And whirring thence, as if alarmed, deceive
The unfeeling schoolboy. Hence, around the head
Of wandering swain, the white-winged plover wheels
Her sounding flight, and then directly on
In long excursion skims the level lawn
To tempt him from her nest. The wild-duck, hence,
O'er the rough moss, and o'er the trackless waste
The heath-hen flutters, pious fraud! to lead
The hot pursuing spaniel far astray.

Be not the muse ashamed here to bemoan
Her brothers of the grove by tyrant man
Inhuman caught, and in the narrow cage
From liberty confined, and boundless air.
Dull are the pretty slaves, their plumage dull,
Ragged, and all its brightening lustre lost;
Nor is that sprightly wildness in their notes,
Which, clear and vigorous, warbles from the beech.
Oh then, ye friends of love and love-taught song,
Spare the soft tribes, this barbarous art forbear!
If on your bosom innocence can win,
Music engage, or piety persuade.

But let not chief the nightingale lament
Her ruined care, too delicately framed
To brook the harsh confinement of the cage.
Oft when, returning with her loaded bill,
The astonished mother finds a vacant nest,
By the hard hand of unrelenting clowns
Robbed, to the ground the vain provision falls;
Her pinions ruffle, and, low-drooping, scarce
Can bear the mourner to the poplar shade;
Where, all abandoned to despair, she sings
Her sorrows through the night, and, on the bough
Sole-sitting, still at every dying fall
Takes up again her lamentable strain

Of winding woe, till wide around the woods
Sigh to her song and with her wail resound.

But now the feathered youth their former bounds,
Ardent, disdain; and, weighing oft their wings,

Demand the free possession of the sky.
This one glad office more, and then dissolves
Parental love at once, now needless grown:
Unlavish Wisdom never works in vain.
'Tis on some evening, sunny, grateful, mild,
When nought but balm is breathing through the woods
With yellow lustre bright, that the new tribes
Visit the spacious heavens, and look abroad
On Nature's common, far as they can see
Or wing, their range and pasture. O'er the boughs
Dancing about, still at the giddy verge
Their resolution fails; their pinions still,
In loose libration stretched, to trust the void
Trembling refuse-till down before them fly
The parent-guides, and chide, exhort, command,
Or push them off. The surging air receives
The plumy burden; and their self-taught wings
Winnow the waving element. On ground
Alighted, bolder up again they lead,
Farther and farther on, the lengthening flight;
Till, vanished every fear, and every power
Roused into life and action, light in air
The acquitted parents see their soaring race,
And, once rejoicing, never know them more.

High from the summit of a craggy cliff,
Hung o'er the deep, such as amazing frowns
On utmost Kilda' shore, whose lonely race
Resign the setting sun to Indian worlds,
The royal eagle draws his vigorous young,
Strong-pounced, and ardent with paternal fire.
Now fit to raise a kingdom of their own,
He drives them from his fort, the towering seat
For ages of his empire-which in peace
Unstained he holds, while many a league to sea
He wings his course, and preys in distant isles.

Should I my steps turn to the rural seat
Whose lofty elms and venerable oaks
Invite the rook, who high amid the boughs
In early Spring his airy city builds,
And ceaseless caws amusive; there, well-pleased,
I might the various polity survey
Of the mixed household-kind. The careful hen
Calls all her chirping family around,
Fed and defended by the fearless cock,
Whose breast with ardour flames, as on he walks
Graceful, and crows defiance. In the pond

The finely-checkered duck before her train
Rows garrulous. The stately-sailing swan
Gives out his snowy plumage to the gale,
And, arching proud his neck, with oary feet
Bears forward fierce, and guards his osier-isle,
Protective of his young. The turkey nigh,
Loud-threatening, reddens; while the peacock spreads
His every-coloured glory to the sun,
And swims in radiant majesty along.
O'er the whole homely scene the cooing dove
Flies thick in amorous chase, and wanton rolls
The glancing eye, and turns the changeful neck.

While thus the gentle tenants of the shade
Indulge their purer loves, the rougher world
Of brutes below rush furious into flame
And fierce desire. Through all his lusty veins
The bull, deep-scorched, the raging passion feels.
Of pasture sick, and negligent of food,
Scarce seen he wades among the yellow broom,
While o'er his ample sides the rambling sprays
Luxuriant shoot; or through the mazy wood
Dejected wanders, nor the enticing bud
Crops, though it presses on his careless sense.
And oft, in jealous maddening fancy wrapt,
He seeks the fight; and, idly-butting, feigns
His rival gored in every knotty trunk.
Him should he meet, the bellowing war begins:
Their eyes flash fury; to the hollowed earth,
Whence the sand flies, they mutter bloody deeds,
And, groaning deep, the impetuous battle mix:
While the fair heifer, balmy-breathing near,
Stands kindling up their rage. The trembling steed,
With this hot impulse seized in every nerve,
Nor heeds the rein, nor hears the sounding thong;
Blows are not felt; but, tossing high his head,
And by the well-known joy to distant plains
Attracted strong, all wild he bursts away;
O'er rocks, and woods, and craggy mountains flies;
And, neighing, on the aerial summit takes
The exciting gale; then, steep-descending, cleaves
The headlong torrents foaming down the hills,
Even where the madness of the straitened stream
Turns in black eddies round: such is the force
With which his frantic heart and sinews swell.

Nor undelighted by the boundless Spring
Are the broad monsters of the foaming deep:

From the deep ooze and gelid cavern roused,
They flounce and tumble in unwieldy joy.
Dire were the strain and dissonant to sing
The cruel raptures of the savage kind:
How, by this flame their native wrath sublimed,
They roam, amid the fury of their heart,
The far-resounding waste in fiercer bands,
And growl their horrid loves. But this the theme
I sing enraptured to the British fair
Forbids, and leads me to the mountain-brow
Where sits the shepherd on the grassy turf,
Inhaling healthful the descending sun.
Around him feeds his many-bleating flock,
Of various cadence; and his sportive lambs,
This way and that convolved in friskful glee,
Their frolics play. And now the sprightly race
Invites them forth; when swift, the signal given,
They start away, and sweep the massy mound
That runs around the hill-the rampart once
Of iron war, in ancient barbarous times,
When disunited Britain ever bled,
Lost in eternal broil, ere yet she grew
To this deep-laid indissoluble state
Where wealth and commerce lift the golden head,
And o'er our labours liberty and law
Impartial watch, the wonder of a world!

What is this mighty breath, ye curious, say,
That in a powerful language, felt, not heard,
Instructs the fowls of heaven, and through their breast
These arts of love diffuses? What, but God?
Inspiring God! who, boundless spirit all
And unremitting energy, pervades,
Adjusts, sustains, and agitates the whole.
He ceaseless works alone, and yet alone
Seems not to work; with such perfection framed
Is this complex, stupendous scheme of things.
But, though concealed, to every purer eye
The informing Author in his works appears:
Chief, lovely Spring, in thee and thy soft scenes
The smiling God is seen-while water, earth,
And air attest his bounty, which exalts
The brute-creation to this finer thought,
And annual melts their undesigning hearts
Profusely thus in tenderness and joy.

Still let my song a nobler note assume,
And sing the infusive force of Spring on man;

When heaven and earth, as if contending, vie
To raise his being and serene his soul.
Can he forbear to join the general smile
Of Nature? Can fierce passions vex his breast,
While every gale is peace, and every grove Is melody?
Hence! from the bounteous walks
Of flowing Spring, ye sordid sons of earth,
Hard, and unfeeling of another's woe,
Or only lavish to yourselves-away!
But come, ye generous minds, in whose wide thought,
Of all his works, Creative Bounty burns
With warmest beam, and on your open front
And liberal eye sits, from his dark retreat
Inviting modest Want. Nor till invoked
Can restless Goodness wait; your active search
Leaves no cold wintry corner unexplored;
Like silent-working Heaven, surprising oft
The lonely heart with unexpected good.
For you the roving spirit of the wind
Blows Spring abroad; for you the teeming clouds
Descend in gladsome plenty o'er the world;
And the Sun sheds his kindest rays for you,
Ye flower of human race! In these green days;
Reviving Sickness lifts her languid head;
Life flows afresh; and young-eyed Health exalts
The whole creation round. Contentment walks
The sunny glade, and feels an inward bliss
Spring o'er his mind, beyond the power of kings
To purchase. Pure Serenity apace
Induces thought, and contemplation still.
By swift degrees the love of nature works,
And warms the bosom; till at last, sublimed
To rapture and enthusiastic heat,
We feel the present Deity, and taste
The joy of God to see a happy world!

These are the sacred feelings of thy heart,
Thy heart informed by reason's purer ray,
O Lyttelton, the friend! Thy passions thus
And meditations vary, as at large,
Courting the muse, through Hagley Park you stray—
Thy British Tempe! There along the dale
With woods o'erhung, and shagged with mossy rocks
Whence on each hand the gushing waters play,
And down the rough cascade white-dashing fall
Or gleam in lengthened vista through the trees,
You silent steal; or sit beneath the shade
Of solemn oaks, that tuft the swelling mounts

Thrown graceful round by Nature's careless hand,
And pensive listen to the various voice
Of rural peace-the herds, the flocks, the birds,
The hollow-whispering breeze, the plaint of rills,
That, purling down amid the twisted roots
Which creep around, their dewy murmurs shake
On the soothed ear. From these abstracted oft,
You wander through the philosophic world;
Where in bright train continual wonders rise
Or to the curious or the pious eye.
And oft, conducted by historic truth,
You tread the long extent of backward time,
Planning with warm benevolence of mind
And honest zeal, unwarped by party-rage,
Britannia's weal,-how from the venal gulf
To raise her virtue and her arts revive.
Or, turning thence thy view, these graver thoughts
The muses charm-while, with sure taste refined,
You draw the inspiring breath of ancient song,
Till nobly rises emulous thy own.
Perhaps thy loved Lucinda shares thy walk,
With soul to thine attuned. Then Nature all
Wears to the lover's eye a look of love;
And all the tumult of a guilty world,
Tost by ungenerous passions, sinks away.
The tender heart is animated peace;
And, as it pours its copious treasures forth
In varied converse, softening every theme,
You, frequent pausing, turn, and from her eyes,
Where meekened sense and amiable grace
And lively sweetness dwell, enraptured drink
That nameless spirit of ethereal joy,
Inimitable happiness! which love
Alone bestows, and on a favoured few.
Meantime you gain the height, from whose fair brow
The bursting prospect spreads immense around;
And, snatched o'er hill and dale, and wood and lawn,
And verdant field, and darkening heath between.
And villages embosomed soft in trees,
And spiry towns by surging columns marked
Of household smoke, your eye excursive roams
Wide-stretching from the Hall in whose kind haunt
The hospitable Genius lingers still,
To where the broken landscape, by degrees
Ascending, roughens into rigid hills
O'er which the Cambrian mountains, like far clouds
That skirt the blue horizon, dusky rise.

Flushed by the spirit of the genial year,
Now from the virgin's cheek a fresher bloom
Shoots less and less the live carnation round;
Her lips blush deeper sweets; she breathes of youth;
The shining moisture swells into her eyes
In brighter flow; her wishing bosom heaves
With palpitations wild; kind tumults seize
Her veins, and all her yielding soul is love.
From the keen gaze her lover turns away,
Full of the dear ecstatic power, and sick
With sighing languishment. Ah then, ye fair!
Be greatly cautious of your sliding hearts:
Dare not the infectious sigh; the pleading look,
Downcast and low, in meek submission dressed,
But full of guile. Let not the fervent tongue,
Prompt to deceive with adulation smooth,
Gain on your purposed will. Nor in the bower
Where woodbines flaunt and roses shed a couch,
While evening draws her crimson curtains round,
Trust your soft minutes with betraying man.
And let the aspiring youth beware of love,
Of the smooth glance beware; for 'tis too late,
When on his heart the torrent-softness pours.
Then wisdom prostrate lies, and fading fame
Dissolves in air away; while the fond soul,
Wrapt in gay visions of unreal bliss,
Still paints the illusive form, the kindling grace,
The enticing smile, the modest-seeming eye,
Beneath whose beauteous beams, belying Heaven,
Lurk searchless cunning, cruelty, and death:
And still, false-warbling in his cheated ear,
Her siren voice enchanting draws him on
To guileful shores and meads of fatal joy.

Even present, in the very lap of love
Inglorious laid-while music flows around,
Perfumes, and oils, and wine, and wanton hours—
Amid the roses fierce repentance rears
Her snaky crest: a quick-returning pang
Shoots through the conscious heart, where honour still
And great design, against the oppressive load
Of luxury, by fits, impatient heave.

But absent, what fantastic woes, aroused,
Rage in each thought, by restless musing fed,
Chill the warm cheek, and blast the bloom of life!
Neglected fortune flies; and, sliding swift,
Prone into ruin fall his scorned affairs.

'Tis nought but gloom around: the darkened sun
Loses his light. The rosy-bosomed Spring
To weeping fancy pines; and yon bright arch,
Contracted, bends into a dusky vault.
All Nature fades extinct; and she alone
Heard, felt, and seen, possesses every thought,
Fills every sense, and pants in every vein.
Books are but formal dulness, tedious friends;
And sad amid the social band he sits,
Lonely and unattentive. From the tongue
The unfinish'd period falls: while, borne away
On swelling thought, his wafted spirit flies
To the vain bosom of his distant fair;
And leaves the semblance of a lover, fixed
In melancholy site, with head declined,
And love-dejected eyes. Sudden he starts,
Shook from his tender trance, and restless runs
To glimmering shades and sympathetic glooms,
Where the dun umbrage o'er the falling stream
Romantic hangs; there through the pensive dusk
Strays, in heart-thrilling meditation lost,
Indulging all to love-or on the bank
Thrown, amid drooping lilies, swells the breeze
With sighs unceasing, and the brook with tears.
Thus in soft anguish he consumes the day,
Nor quits his deep retirement till the moon
Peeps through the chambers of the fleecy east,
Enlightened by degrees, and in her train
Leads on the gentle hours; then forth he walks,
Beneath the trembling languish of her beam,
With softened soul, and woos the bird of eve
To mingle woes with his; or, while the world
And all the sons of care lie hushed in sleep,
Associates with the midnight shadows drear,
And, sighing to the lonely taper, pours
His idly-tortured heart into the page
Meant for the moving messenger of love,
Where rapture burns on rapture, every line
With rising frenzy fired. But if on bed
Delirious flung, sleep from his pillow flies.
All night he tosses, nor the balmy power
In any posture finds; till the grey morn
Lifts her pale lustre on the paler wretch,
Exanimate by love-and then perhaps
Exhausted nature sinks a while to rest,
Still interrupted by distracted dreams
That o'er the sick imagination rise
And in black colours paint the mimic scene.

Oft with the enchantress of his soul he talks;
Sometimes in crowds distressed; or, if retired
To secret-winding flower-enwoven bowers,
Far from the dull impertinence of man,
Just as he, credulous, his endless cares
Begins to lose in blind oblivious love,
Snatched from her yielded hand, he knows not how,
Through forests huge, and long untravelled heaths
With desolation brown, he wanders waste,
In night and tempest wrapt; or shrinks aghast
Back from the bending precipice; or wades
The turbid stream below, and strives to reach
The farther shore where, succourless and sad,
She with extended arms his aid implores,
But strives in vain: borne by the outrageous flood
To distance down, he rides the ridgy wave,
Or whelmed beneath the boiling eddy sinks.

These are the charming agonies of love,
Whose misery delights. But through the heart
Should jealousy its venom once diffuse,
'Tis then delightful misery no more,
But agony unmixed, incessant gall,
Corroding every thought, and blasting all
Love's Paradise. Ye fairy prospects, then,
Ye bed of roses and ye bowers of joy,
Farewell! Ye gleamings of departed peace,
Shine out your last! The yellow-tinging plague
Internal vision taints, and in a night
Of livid gloom imagination wraps.
Ah then! instead of love-enlivened cheeks,
Of sunny features, and of ardent eyes
With flowing rapture bright, dark looks succeed,
Suffused, and glaring with untender fire,
A clouded aspect, and a burning cheek
Where the whole poisoned soul malignant sits,
And frightens love away. Ten thousand fears
Invented wild, ten thousand frantic views
Of horrid rivals hanging on the charms
For which he melts in fondness, eat him up
With fervent anguish and consuming rage.
In vain reproaches lend their idle aid,
Deceitful pride, and resolution frail,
Giving false peace a moment. Fancy pours
Afresh her beauties on his busy thought,
Her first endearments twining round the soul
With all the witchcraft of ensnaring love.
Straight the fierce storm involves his mind anew,

Flames through the nerves, and boils along the veins;
While anxious doubt distracts the tortured heart:
For even the sad assurance of his fears
Were peace to what he feels. Thus the warm youth,
Whom love deludes into his thorny wilds
Through flowery-tempting paths, or leads a life
Of fevered rapture or of cruel care—
His brightest aims extinguished all, and all
His lively moments running down to waste.

But happy they! the happiest of their kind!
Whom gentler stars unite, and in one fate
Their hearts, their fortunes, and their beings blend.
'Tis not the coarser tie of human laws,
Unnatural oft, and foreign to the mind,
That binds their peace, but harmony itself,
Attuning all their passions into love;
Where friendship full-exerts her softest power,
Perfect esteem enlivened by desire
Ineffable and sympathy of soul,
Thought meeting thought, and will preventing will,
With boundless confidence: for nought but love
Can answer love, and render bliss secure.
Let him, ungenerous, who, alone intent
To bless himself, from sordid parents buys
The loathing virgin, in eternal care
Well-merited consume his nights and days;
Let barbarous nations, whose inhuman love
Is wild desire, fierce as the suns they feel;
Let eastern tyrants from the light of heaven
Seclude their bosom-slaves, meanly possessed
Of a mere lifeless, violated form:
While those whom love cements in holy faith
And equal transport free as nature live,
Disdaining fear. What is the world to them,
Its pomp, its pleasure, and its nonsense all,
Who in each other clasp whatever fair
High fancy forms, and lavish hearts can wish?
Something than beauty dearer, should they look
Or on the mind or mind-illumined face;
Truth, goodness, honour, harmony, and love,
The richest bounty of indulgent Heaven
Meantime a smiling offspring rises round,
And mingles both their graces. By degrees
The human blossom blows; and every day,
Soft as it rolls along, shows some new charm,
The father's lustre and the mother's bloom.
Then infant reason grows apace, and calls

For the kind hand of an assiduous care.
Delightful task! to rear the tender thought,
To teach the young idea how to shoot,
To pour the fresh instruction o'er the mind,
To breathe the enlivening spirit, and to fix
The generous purpose in the glowing breast.
Oh, speak the joy! ye, whom the sudden tear
Surprises often, while you look around,
And nothing strikes your eye but sights of bliss,
All various Nature pressing on the heart—
An elegant sufficiency, content,
Retirement, rural quiet, friendship, books,
Ease and alternate labour, useful life,
Progressive virtue, and approving Heaven!
These are the matchless joys of virtuous love;
And thus their moments fly. The Seasons thus,
As ceaseless round a jarring world they roll,
Still find them happy; and consenting Spring
Sheds her own rosy garland on their heads:
Till evening comes at last, serene and mild;
When after the long vernal day of life,
Enamoured more, as more remembrance swells,
With many a proof of recollected love,
Together down they sink in social sleep;
Together freed, their gentle spirits fly
To scenes where love and bliss immortal reign.

SUMMER

THE ARGUMENT

The subject proposed. Invocation. Address to Mr. Dodington. An introductory reflection on the motion of the heavenly bodies; whence the succession of the Seasons. As the face of nature in this season is almost uniform, the progress of the poem is a description of a Summer's day. The dawn. Sun-rising. Hymn to the sun. Forenoon. Summer insects described. Hay-making. Sheep-shearing. Noonday. A woodland retreat. Group of herds and flocks. A solemn grove: how it affects a contemplative mind. A cataract, and rude scene. View of Summer in the torrid zone. Storm of thunder and lightning. A tale. The storm over. A serene afternoon. Bathing. Hour of walking. Transition to the prospect of a rich, well-cultivated country; which introduces a panegyric on Great Britain. Sunset. Evening. Night. Summer meteors. A comet. The whole concluding with the praise of philosophy.

From brightening fields of ether fair-disclosed,
Child of the sun, refulgent Summer comes
In pride of youth, and felt through nature's depth:
He comes, attended by the sultry hours

And ever-fanning breezes on his way;
While from his ardent look the turning Spring
Averts her blushful face, and earth and skies
All-smiling to his hot dominion leaves.
Hence let me haste into the mid-wood shade,
Where scarce a sunbeam wanders through the gloom,
And on the dark-green grass, beside the brink
Of haunted stream that by the roots of oak
Rolls o'er the rocky channel, lie at large
And sing the glories of the circling year.

Come, Inspiration! from thy hermit-seat,
By mortal seldom found: may fancy dare,
From thy fixed serious eye and raptured glance
Shot on surrounding Heaven, to steal one look
Creative of the poet, every power
Exalting to an ecstasy of soul.
And thou, my youthful Muse's early friend,
In whom the human graces all unite—

Pure light of mind and tenderness of heart,
Jenius and wisdom, the gay social sense
By decency chastised, goodness and wit
In seldom-meeting harmony combined,
Unblemished honour, and an active zeal
For Britain's glory, liberty, and man:

O Dodington! attend my rural song,
Stoop to my theme, inspirit every line,
And teach me to deserve thy just applause.

With what an awful world-revolving power
Were first the unwieldy planets launched along
The illimitable void!-thus to remain,
Amid the flux of many thousand years
That oft has swept the toiling race of men,
And all their laboured monuments away,
Firm, unremitting, matchless in their course;
To the kind-tempered change of night and day,
And of the seasons ever stealing round,
Minutely faithful: such the all-perfect Hand
That poised, impels, and rules the steady whole!

When now no more the alternate Twins are fired,
And Cancer reddens with the solar blaze,
Short is the doubtful empire of the night;
And soon, observant of approaching day,
The meek-eyed morn appears, mother of dews,

At first faint-gleaming in the dappled east;
Till far o'er ether spreads the widening glow,
And, from before the lustre of her face,
White break the clouds away. With quickened step,
Brown night retires. Young day pours in apace,
And opens all the lawny prospect wide.
The dripping rock, the mountain's misty top
Swell on the sight and brighten with the dawn.
Blue through the dusk the smoking currents shine;
And from the bladed field the fearful hare
Limps awkward; while along the forest glade
The wild deer trip, and often turning gaze
At early passenger. Music awakes,
The native voice of undissembled joy;
And thick around the woodland hymns arise.
Roused by the cock, the soon-clad shepherd leaves
His mossy cottage, where with peace he dwells,
And from the crowded fold in order drives
His flock to taste the verdure of the morn.

Falsely luxurious, will not man awake,
And, springing from the bed of sloth, enjoy
The cool, the fragrant, and the silent hour,
To meditation due and sacred song?
For is there aught in sleep can charm the wise?
To lie in dead oblivion, losing half
The fleeting moments of too short a life—
Total extinction of the enlightened soul!
Or else, to feverish vanity alive,
Wildered, and tossing through distempered dreams!
Who would in such a gloomy state remain
Longer than nature craves; when every muse
And every blooming pleasure wait without
To bless the wildly-devious morning walk?

But yonder comes the powerful king of day
Rejoicing in the east. The lessening cloud,
The kindling azure, and the mountain's brow
Illumed with fluid gold, his near approach
Betoken glad. Lo! now, apparent all,
Aslant the dew-bright earth and coloured air,
He looks in boundless majesty abroad,
And sheds the shining day, that burnished plays
On rocks, and hills, and towers, and wandering streams
High-gleaming from afar. Prime cheerer, Light!
Of all material beings first and best!
Efflux divine! Nature's resplendent robe,
Without whose vesting beauty all were wrapt

In unessential gloom; and thou, O Sun!
Soul of surrounding worlds! in whom best seen
Shines out thy Maker! may I sing of thee?

'Tis by thy secret, strong, attractive force,
As with a chain indissoluble bound,
Thy system rolls entire-from the far bourne
Of utmost Saturn, wheeling wide his round
Of thirty years, to Mercury, whose disk
Can scarce be caught by philosophic eye,
Lost in the near effulgence of thy blaze.

Informer of the planetary train!
Without whose quickening glance their cumbrous orbs
Were brute unlovely mass, inert and dead,
And not, as now, the green abodes of life!
How many forms of being wait on thee,
Inhaling spirit, from the unfettered mind,
By thee sublimed, down to the daily race,
The mixing myriads of thy setting beam!

The vegetable world is also thine,
Parent of Seasons! who the pomp precede
That waits thy throne, as through thy vast domain,
Annual, along the bright ecliptic road
In world-rejoicing state it moves sublime.
Meantime the expecting nations, circled gay
With all the various tribes of foodful earth,
Implore thy bounty, or send grateful up
A common hymn: while, round thy beaming car,
High-seen, the Seasons lead, in sprightly dance
Harmonious knit, the rosy-fingered hours,
The zephyrs floating loose, the timely rains,
Of bloom ethereal the light-footed dews,
And, softened into joy, the surly storms.
These, in successive turn, with lavish hand
Shower every beauty, every fragrance shower,
Herbs, flowers, and fruits; till, kindling at thy touch,
From land to land is flushed the vernal year.

Nor to the surface of enlivened earth,
Graceful with hills and dales, and leafy woods,
Her liberal tresses, is thy force confined;
But, to the bowelled cavern darting deep,
The mineral kinds confess thy mighty power.
Effulgent hence the veiny marble shines;
Hence labour draws his tools; hence burnished war
Gleams on the day; the nobler works of peace

Hence bless mankind; and generous commerce binds
The round of nations in a golden chain.

The unfruitful rock itself, impregned by thee,
In dark retirement forms the lucid stone.
The lively diamond drinks thy purest rays,
Collected light compact; that, polished bright,
And all its native lustre let abroad,
Dares, as it sparkles on the fair one's breast,
With vain ambition emulate her eyes.
At thee the ruby lights its deepening glow,
And with a waving radiance inward flames.
From thee the sapphire, solid ether, takes
Its hue cerulean; and, of evening tinct,
The purple-streaming amethyst is thine
With thy own smile the yellow topaz burns;
Nor deeper verdure dyes the robe of Spring
When first she gives it to the southern gale
Than the green emerald shows. But, all combined,
Thick through the whitening opal play thy beams;
Or, flying several from its surface, form
A trembling variance of revolving hues
As the site varies in the gazer's hand.

The very dead creation from thy touch
Assumes a mimic life. By thee refined,
In brighter mazes the relucent stream
Plays o'er the mead. The precipice abrupt,
Projecting horror on the blackened flood,
Softens at thy return. The desert joys
Wildly through all his melancholy bounds.
Rude ruins glitter; and the briny deep,
Seen from some pointed promontory's top
Far to the blue horizon's utmost verge,
Restless reflects a floating gleam. But this,
And all the much-transported Muse can sing,
Are to thy beauty, dignity, and use
Unequal far, great delegated Source
Of light and life and grace and joy below!

How shall I then attempt to sing of Him
Who, Light Himself, in uncreated light
Invested deep, dwells awfully retired
From mortal eye or angel's purer ken;
Whose single smile has, from the first of time,
Filled overflowing all those lamps of heaven
That beam for ever through the boundless sky:
But, should He hide his face, the astonished sun

And all the extinguished stars would, loosening, reel
Wide from their spheres, and chaos come again.

And yet, was every faltering tongue of man,
Almighty Father! silent in thy praise,
Thy works themselves would raise a general voice;
Even in the depth of solitary woods,
By human foot untrod, proclaim thy power;
And to the quire celestial Thee resound,
The eternal cause, support, and end of all!

To me be Nature's volume broad displayed;
And to peruse its all-instructing page,
Or, haply catching inspiration thence,
Some easy passage, raptured, to translate,
My sole delight; as through the falling glooms
Pensive I stray, or with the rising dawn
On fancy's eagle-wing excursive soar.

Now, flaming up the heavens, the potent sun
Melts into limpid air the high-raised clouds
And morning fogs that hovered round the hills
In parti-coloured bands; till wide unveiled
The face of nature shines from where earth seems,
Far-stretched around, to meet the bending sphere.

Half in a blush of clustering roses lost,
Dew-dropping Coolness to the shade retires;
There, on the verdant turf or flowery bed,
By gelid founts and careless rills to muse;
While tyrant Heat, dispreading through the sky
With rapid sway, his burning influence darts
On man and beast and herb and tepid stream.

Who can unpitying see the flowery race,
Shed by the morn, their new-flushed bloom resign
Before the parching beam? So fade the fair,
When fevers revel through their azure veins.
But one, the lofty follower of the sun,
Sad when he sets, shuts up her yellow leaves,
Drooping all night; and, when he warm returns,
Points her enamoured bosom to his ray.

Home from his morning task the swain retreats,
His flock before him stepping to the fold;
While the full-uddered mother lows around
The cheerful cottage then expecting food,
The food of innocence and health! The daw,

The rook, and magpie, to the grey-grown oaks
(That the calm village in their verdant arms,
Sheltering, embrace) direct their lazy flight;
Where on the mingling boughs they sit embowered
All the hot noon, till cooler hours arise.
Faint underneath the household fowls convene;
And, in a corner of the buzzing shade,
The house-dog with the vacant greyhound lies
Out-stretched and sleepy. In his slumbers one
Attacks the nightly thief, and one exults
O'er hill and dale; till, wakened by the wasp,
They starting snap. Nor shall the muse disdain
To let the little noisy summer-race
Live in her lay and flutter through her song:
Not mean though simple-to the sun allied,
From him they draw their animating fire.

Waked by his warmer ray, the reptile young
Come winged abroad, by the light air upborne,
Lighter, and full of soul. From every chink
And secret corner, where they slept away
The wintry storms, or rising from their tombs
To higher life, by myriads forth at once
Swarming they pour, of all the varied hues
Their beauty-beaming parent can disclose.
Ten thousand forms, ten thousand different tribes
People the blaze. To sunny waters some
By fatal instinct fly; where on the pool
They sportive wheel, or, sailing down the stream,
Are snatched immediate by the quick-eyed trout
Or darting salmon. Through the green-wood glade
Some love to stray; there lodged, amused, and fed
In the fresh leaf. Luxurious, others make
The meads their choice, and visit every flower
And every latent herb: for the sweet task
To propagate their kinds, and where to wrap
In what soft beds their young, yet undisclosed,
Employs their tender care. Some to the house,
The fold, and dairy hungry bend their flight;
Sip round the pail, or taste the curdling cheese:
Oft, inadvertent, from the milky stream
They meet their fate; or, weltering in the bowl,
With powerless wings around them wrapt, expire.

But chief to heedless flies the window proves
A constant death; where, gloomily retired,
The villain spider lives, cunning and fierce,
Mixture abhorred! Amid a mangled heap

Of carcases in eager watch he sits,
 O'erlooking all his waving snares around.
Near the dire cell the dreadless wanderer oft
Passes; as oft the ruffian shows his front.
The prey at last ensnared, he dreadful darts
With rapid glide along the leaning line;
And, fixing in the wretch his cruel fangs,
Strikes backward grimly pleased: the fluttering wing
And shriller sound declare extreme distress,
And ask the helping hospitable hand.

Resounds the living surface of the ground:
Nor undelightful is the ceaseless hum
To him who muses through the woods at noon,
Or drowsy shepherd as he lies reclined,
With half-shut eyes, beneath the floating shade
Of willows grey, close-crowding o'er the brook.

Gradual from these what numerous kinds descend,
Evading even the microscopic eye!
Full Nature swarms with life; one wondrous mass
Of animals, or atoms organized
Waiting the vital breath when Parent-Heaven
Shall bid his spirit blow. The hoary fen
In putrid streams emits the living cloud
Of pestilence. Through subterranean cells,
Where searching sunbeams scarce can find a way,
Earth animated heaves. The flowery leaf
Wants not its soft inhabitants. Secure
Within its winding citadel the stone
Holds multitudes. But chief the forest boughs,
That dance unnumbered to the playful breeze,
The downy orchard, and the melting pulp
Of mellow fruit the nameless nations feed
Of evanescent insects. Where the pool
Stands mantled o'er with green, invisible
Amid the floating verdure millions stray.
Each liquid too, whether it pierces, soothes,
Inflames, refreshes, or exalts the taste,
With various forms abounds. Nor is the stream
Of purest crystal, nor the lucid air,
Though one transparent vacancy it seems,
Void of their unseen people. These, concealed
By the kind art of forming Heaven, escape
The grosser eye of man: for, if the worlds
In worlds inclosed should on his senses burst,

From cates ambrosial and the nectared bowl

He would abhorrent turn; and in dead night,
When Silence sleeps o'er all, be stunned with noise.

Let no presuming impiouis railer tax
Creative Wisdom, as if aught was formed
In vain, or not for admirabl eneds.
Shall little haughty Ignorance pronounce
His works unwise, of which the smallest part
Exceeds the narrow vision of her mind?
As if upon a full-proportioned dome,
On swelling columns heaved, the pride of art
A critic fly, whose feeble ray scarce spreads
An inch around, with blind presumption bold
Should dare to tax the structure of the whole.

And lives the man whose universal eye
Has swept at once the unbounded scheme of things,
Marked their dependence so and firm accord,
As with unfaltering accent to conclude
That this availeth nought? Has any seen
The mighty chain of beings, lessening down
From infinite perfection to the brink
Of dreary nothing, desolate abyss!
From which astonished thought recoiling turns?
Till then, alone let zealous praise ascend
And hymns of holy wonder to that Power
Whose wisdom shines as lovely on our minds
As on our smiling eyes his servant-sun.

Thick in yon stream of light, a thousand ways,
Upward and downward, thwarting an convolved,
The quivering nations sport; till, tempest-winged,
Fierce Winter sweeps them from the face of day.
Even so luxurious men, unheeding, pass
An idle summer life in fortune's shine,
A season's glitter! Thus they flutter on
From toy to toy, from vanity to vice;
Till, blown away by death, oblivion comes
Behind and strikes them from the book of life.

Now swarms the village o'er the jovial mead—
The rustic youth, brown with meridian toil,
Healthful and strong; full as the summer rose
Blown by prevailing suns, the ruddy maid,
Half naked, swelling on the sight, and all
Her kindled graces burning o'er her cheek.
Even stooping age is here; and infant hands
Trail the long rake, or, with the fragrant load

O'ercharged, amid the kind oppression roll.
Wide flies the tedded grain; all in a row
Advancing broad, or wheeling round the field,
They spread their breathing harvest to the sun,
That throws refreshful round a rural smell;
Or, as they rake the green-appearing ground,
And drive the dusky wave along the mead,
The russet hay-cock rises thick behind
In order gay: while heard from dale to dale,
Waking the breeze, resounds the blended voice
Of happy labour, love, and social glee.

Or, rushing thence, in one diffusive band
They drive the troubled flocks, by many a dog
Compelled, to where the mazy-running brook
Forms a deep pool, this bank abrupt and high,
And that fair-spreading in a pebbled shore.
Urged to the giddy brink, much is the toil,
The clamour much of men and boys and dogs
Ere the soft, fearful people to the flood
Commit their woolly sides. And oft the swain,
On some impatient seizing, hurls them in:
Emboldened then, nor hesitating more,
Fast, fast they plunge amid the flashing wave,
And, panting, labour to the farther shore.
Repeated this, till deep the well-washed fleece
Has drunk the flood, and from his lively haunt
The trout is banished by the sordid stream.
Heavy and dripping, to the breezy brow
Slow move the harmless race; where, as they spread
Their swelling treasures to the sunny ray,
Inly disturbed, and wondering what this wild
Outrageous tumult means, their loud complaints
The country fill; and, tossed from rock to rock,
Incessant bleatings run around the hills.
At last, of snowy white the gathered flocks
Are in the wattled pen innumerous pressed,
Head above head; and, ranged in lusty rows,
The shepherds sit, and whet the sounding shears.
The housewife waits to roll her fleecy stores,
With all her gay-drest maids attending round.
One, chief, in gracious dignity enthroned,
Shines o'er the rest, the pastoral queen, and rays
Her smiles sweet-beaming on her shepherd-king;
While the glad circle round them yield their souls
To festive mirth, and wit that knows no gall.
Meantime, their joyous task goes on apace:
Some mingling stir the melted tar, and some,

Deep on the new-shorn vagrant's heaving side
To stamp his master's cipher ready stand;
Others the unwilling wether drag along;
And, glorying in his might, the sturdy boy
Holds by the twisted horns the indignant ram.
Behold where bound, and of its robe bereft
By needy man, that all-depending lord,
How meek, how patient, the mild creature lies!
What softness in its melancholy face,
What dumb complaining innocence appears!
Fear not, ye gentle tribes! 'tis not the knife
Of horrid slaughter that is o'er you waved;
No, 'tis the tender swain's well-guided shears,
Who having now, to pay his annual care,
Borrowed your fleece, to you a cumbrous load,
Will send you bounding to your hills again.

A simple scene! yet hence Britannia sees
Her solid grandeur rise: hence she commands
The exalted stores of every brighter clime,
The treasures of the sun without his rage:
Hence, fervent all with culture; toil, and arts,
Wide glows her land: her dreadful thunder hence
Rides o'er the waves sublime, and now, even now,
Impending hangs o'er Gallia's humbled coast;
Hence rules the circling deep, and awes the world.

'Tis raging noon; and, vertical, the sun
Darts on the head direct his forceful rays.
O'er heaven and earth, far as the ranging eye
Can sweep, a dazzling deluge reigns; and all
From pole to pole is undistinguished blaze.
In vain the sight dejected to the ground
Stoops for relief; thence hot ascending steams
And keen reflection pain. Deep to the root
Of vegetation parched, the cleaving fields
And slippery lawn an arid hue disclose,
Blast fancy's blooms, and wither even the soul.
Echo no more returns the cheerful sound
Of sharpening scythe: the mower, sinking, heaps
O'er him the humid hay, with flowers perfumed;
And scarce a chirping grasshopper is heard
Through the dumb mead. Distressful nature pants.
The very streams look languid from afar,
Or, through the unsheltered glade, impatient seem
To hurl into the covert of the grove.

All-conquering heat, oh, intermit thy wrath!

And on my throbbing temples potent thus
Beam not so fierce! Incessant still you flow,
And still another fervent flood succeeds,
Poured on the head profuse. In vain I sigh,
And restless turn, and look around for night:
Night is far off; and hotter hours approach.
Thrice happy he, who on the sunless side
Of a romantic mountain, forest-crowned,
Beneath the whole collected shade reclines;
Or in the gelid caverns, woodbine-wrought
And fresh bedewed with ever-spouting streams,
Sits coolly calm; while all the world without,
Unsatisfied and sick, tosses in noon.
Emblem instructive of the virtuous man,
Who keeps his tempered mind serene and pure,
And every passion aptly harmonized
Amid a jarring world with vice inflamed.

Welcome, ye shades! ye bowery thickets, hail!
Ye lofty pines! ye venerable oaks!
Ye ashes wild, resounding o'er the steep!
Delicious is your shelter to the soul
As to the hunted hart the sallying spring
Or stream full-flowing, that his swelling sides
Laves as he floats along the herbaged brink.
Cool through the nerves your pleasing comfort glides;
The heart beats glad; the fresh-expanded eye
And ear resume their watch; the sinews knit;
And life shoots swift through all the lightened limbs.

Around the adjoining brook, that purls along
The vocal grove, now fretting o'er a rock,
Now scarcely moving through a reedy pool,
Now starting to a sudden stream, and now
Gently diffused into a limpid plain,
A various group the herds and flocks compose,
Rural confusion! On the grassy bank
Some ruminating lie, while others stand
Half in the flood and, often bending, sip
The circling surface. In the middle droops
The strong laborious ox, of honest front,
Which incomposed he shakes; and from his sides
The troublous insects lashes with his tail,
Returning still. Amid his subjects safe
Slumbers the monarch-swain, his careless arm
Thrown round his head on downy moss sustained;
Here laid his scrip with wholesome viands filled,
There, listening every noise, his watchful dog.

Light fly his slumbers, if perchance a flight
Of angry gad-flies fasten on the herd,
That startling scatters from the shallow brook
In search of lavish stream. Tossing the foam,
They scorn the keeper's voice, and scour the plain
Through all the bright severity of noon;
While from their labouring breasts a hollow moan
Proceeding runs low-bellowing round the hills.

Oft in this season too, the horse, provoked,
While his big sinews full of spirits swell,
Trembling with vigour, in the heat of blood
Springs the high fence, and, o'er the field effused,
Darts on the gloomy flood with steadfast eye
And heart estranged to fear: his nervous chest,
Luxuriant and erect, the seat of strength,
Bears down the opposing stream; quenchless his thirst,
He takes the river at redoubled draughts,
And with wide nostrils, snorting, skims the wave.

Still let me pierce into the midnight depth
Of yonder grove, of wildest largest growth,
That, forming high in air a woodland quire,
Nods o'er the mount beneath. At every step,
Solemn and slow the shadows blacker fall,
And all is awful listening gloom around.

These are the haunts of meditation, these
The scenes where ancient bards the inspiring breath
Ecstatic felt, and, from this world retired,
Conversed with angels and immortal forms,
On gracious errands bent-to save the fall
Of virtue struggling on the brink of vice;
In waking whispers and repeated dreams
To hint pure thought, and warn the favoured soul,
For future trials fated, to prepare;
To prompt the poet, who devoted gives
His muse to better themes; to soothe the pangs
Of dying worth, and from the patriot's breast
(Backward to mingle in detested war,
But foremost when engaged) to turn the death;
And numberless such offices of love,
Daily and nightly, zealous to perform.

Shook sudden from the bosom of the sky,
A thousand shapes or glide athwart the dusk
Or stalk majestic on. Deep-roused, I feel

A sacred terror, a severe delight,
Creep through my mortal frame; and thus, methinks,
A voice, than human more, the abstracted ear
Of fancy strikes-'Be not of us afraid,
Poor kindred man! thy fellow-creatures, we
From the same Parent-Power our beings drew,
The same our Lord and laws and great pursuit.
Once some of us, like thee, through stormy life
Toiled tempest-beaten ere we could attain
This holy calm, this harmony of mind,
Where purity and peace immingle charms.
Then fear not us; but with responsive song,
Amid these dim recesses, undisturbed
By noisy folly and discordant vice,
Of Nature sing with us, and Nature's God.
Here frequent, at the visionary hour,
When musing midnight reigns or silent noon,
Angelic harps are in full concert heard,
And voices chaunting from the wood-crown'd hill,
The deepening dale, or inmost sylvan glade:
A privilege bestow'd by us alone
On contemplation, or the hallow'd ear
Of poet swelling to seraphic strain.'

And art thou, Stanley, of that sacred band?
Alas! for us too soon! Though raised above
The reach of human pain, above the flight
Of human joy, yet with a mingled ray
Of sadly pleased remembrance, must thou feel
A mother's love, a mother's tender woe—
Who seeks thee still in many a former scene,
Seeks thy fair form, thy lovely beaming eyes,
Thy pleasing converse, by gay lively sense
Inspired, where moral wisdom mildly shone
Without the toil of art, and virtue glowed
In all her smiles without forbidding pride.
But, O thou best of parents! wipe thy tears;
Or rather to parental Nature pay
The tears of grateful joy, who for a while
Lent thee this younger self, this opening bloom
Of thy enlightened mind and gentle worth. 580
Believe the muse-the wintry blast of death
Kills not the buds of virtue; no, they spread
Beneath the heavenly beam of brighter suns
Through endless ages into higher powers.

Thus up the mount, in airy vision rapt,
I stray, regardless whither; till the sound

Of a near fall of water every sense
Wakes from the charm of thought: swift-shrinking back,
I check my steps and view the broken scene.

Smooth to the shelving brink a copious flood
Rolls fair and placid; where, collected all
In one impetuous torrent, down the steep
It thundering shoots, and shakes the country round.
At first, an azure sheet, it rushes broad;
Then, whitening by degrees as prone it falls,
And from the loud-resounding rocks below
Dashed in a cloud of foam, it sends aloft
A hoary mist and forms a ceaseless shower.
Nor can the tortured wave here find repose;
But, raging still amid the shaggy rocks,
Now flashes o'er the scattered fragments, now
Aslant the hollow channel rapid darts;
And, falling fast from gradual slope to slope,
With wild infracted course and lessened roar
It gains a safer bed, and steals at last
Along the mazes of the quiet vale.

Invited from the cliff, to whose dark brow
He clings, the steep-ascending eagle soars
With upward pinions through the flood of day,
And, giving full his bosom to the blaze,
Gains on the Sun; while all the tuneful race,
Smit by afflictive noon, disordered droop
Deep in the thicket, or, from bower to bower
Responsive, force an interrupted strain.
The stock-dove only through the forest coos,
Mournfully hoarse; oft ceasing from his plaint,
Short interval of weary woe! again
The sad idea of his murdered mate,
Struck from his side by savage fowler's guile,
Across his fancy comes; and then resounds
A louder song of sorrow through the grove.

Beside the dewy border let me sit,
All in the freshness of the humid air,
There on that hollowed rock, grotesque and wild,
An ample chair moss-lined, and over head
By flowering umbrage shaded; where the bee
Strays diligent, and with the extracted balm
Of fragrant woodbine loads his little thigh.

Now, while I taste the sweetness of the shade,
While Nature lies around deep-lulled in noon,

Now come, bold fancy, spread a daring flight
And view the wonders of the torrid zone:
Climes unrelenting! with whose rage compared,
Yon blaze is feeble and yon skies are cool.

See how at once the bright effulgent sun,
Rising direct, swift chases from the sky
The short-lived twilight, and with ardent blaze
Looks gaily fierce o'er all the dazzling air!
He mounts his throne; but kind before him sends,
Issuing from out the portals of the morn,
The general breeze to mitigate his fire
And breathe refreshment on a fainting world.
Great are the scenes, with dreadful beauty crowned
And barbarous wealth, that see, each circling year,
Returning suns and double seasons pass;
Rocks rich in gems, and mountains big with mines,
That on the high equator ridgy rise,
Whence many a bursting stream auriferous plays;
Majestic woods of every vigorous green,
Stage above stage high waving o'er the hills,
Or to the far horizon wide-diffused,
A boundless deep immensity of shade.

Here lofty trees, to ancient song unknown,
The noble sons of potent heat and floods
Prone-rushing from the clouds, rear high to heaven
Their thorny stems, and broad around them throw
Meridian gloom. Here, in eternal prime,
Unnumbered fruits of keen delicious taste
And vital spirit drink, amid the cliffs
And burning sands that bank the shrubby vales,
Redoubled day, yet in their rugged coats
A friendly juice to cool its rage contain.

Bear me, Pomona! to thy citron groves;
To where the lemon and the piercing lime,
With the deep orange glowing through the green,
Their lighter glories blend. Lay me reclined
Beneath the spreading tamarind, that shakes,
Fanned by the breeze, its fever-cooling fruit.
Deep in the night the massy locust sheds
Quench my hot limbs; or lead me through the maze,
Embowering endless, of the Indian fig;
Or, thrown at gayer ease on some fair brow,
Let me behold, by breezy murmurs cooled,
Broad o'er my head the verdant cedar wave,
And high palmettos lift their graceful shade.

Oh, stretched amid these orchards of the sun,
Give me to drain the cocoa's milky bowl,
And from the palm to draw its freshening wine!
More bounteous far than all the frantic juice
Which Bacchus pours. Nor, on its slender twigs
Low-bending, be the full pomegranate scorned;
Nor, creeping through the woods, the gelid race
Of berries. Oft in humble station dwells
Unboastful worth, above fastidious pomp.
Witness, thou best Anana, thou the pride
Of vegetable life, beyond whate'er
The poets imaged in the golden age:
Quick let me strip thee of thy tufty coat,
Spread thy ambrosial stores, and feast with Jove!

From these the prospect varies. Plains immense
Lie stretched below, interminable meads
And vast savannas, where the wandering eye,
Unfixt, is in a verdant ocean lost.
Another Flora there, of bolder hues
And richer sweets beyond our garden's pride,
Plays o'er the fields, and showers with sudden hand
Exuberant spring-for oft these valleys shift
Their green-embroidered robe to fiery brown,
And swift to green again, as scorching suns
Or streaming dews and torrent rains prevail.
Along these lonely regions, where, retired
From little scenes of art, great Nature dwells
In awful solitude, and naught is seen
But the wild herds that own no master's stall,
Prodigious rivers roll their fattening seas;
On whose luxuriant herbage, half-concealed,
Like a fallen cedar, far diffused his train,
Cased in green scales, the crocodile extends.
The flood disparts: behold! in plaited mail
Behemoth rears his head. Glanced from his side,
The darted steel in idle shivers flies:
He fearless walks the plain, or seeks the hills,
Where, as he crops his varied fare, the herds,
In widening circle round, forget their food
And at the harmless stranger wondering gaze.

Peaceful beneath primeval trees that cast
Their ample shade o'er Niger's yellow stream,
And where the Ganges rolls his sacred wave,
Or mid the central depth of blackening woods,
High-raised in solemn theatre around,
Leans the huge elephant-wisest of brutes!

Oh, truly wise! with gentle might endowed,
Though powerful not destructive! Here he sees
Revolving ages sweep the changeful earth,
And empires rise and fall; regardless he
Of what the never-resting race of men
Project: thrice happy, could he 'scape their guile
Who mine, from cruel avarice, his steps,
Or with his towery grandeur swell their state,
The pride of kings! or else his strength pervert,
And bid him rage amid the mortal fray,
Astonished at the madness of mankind.

Wide o'er the winding umbrage of the floods,
Like vivid blossoms glowing from afar,
Thick-swarm the brighter birds. For nature's hand,
That with a sportive vanity has decked
The plumy nations, there her gayest hues
Profusely pours But, if she bids them shine
Arrayed in all the beauteous beams of day,
Yet, frugal still, she humbles them in song.
Nor envy we the gaudy robes they lent
Proud Montezuma's realm, whose legions cast
A boundless radiance waving on the sun,
While Philomel is ours, while in our shades,
Through the soft silence of the listening night,
The sober-suited songstress trills her lay.

But come, my muse, the desert-barrier burst,
A wild expanse of lifeless sand and sky;
And, swifter than the toiling caravan,
Shoot o'er the vale of Sennar; ardent climb
The Nubian mountains, and the secret bounds
Of jealous Abyssinia boldly pierce.
Thou art no ruffian, who beneath the mask
Of social commerce com'st to rob their wealth;
No holy fury thou, blaspheming Heaven,
With consecrated steel to stab their peace,
And through the land, yet red from civil wounds,
To spread the purple tyranny of Rome.
Thou, like the harmless bee, mayst freely range
From mead to mead bright with exalted flowers,
From jasmine grove to grove; may'st wander gay
Through palmy shades and aromatic woods
That grace the plains, invest the peopled hills,
And up the more than Alpine mountains wave.
There on the breezy summit, spreading fair
For many a league, or on stupendous rocks,
That from the sun-redoubling valley lift,

Cool to the middle air, their lawny tops,
Where palaces and fanes and villas rise,
And gardens smile around and cultured fields,
And fountains gush, and careless herds and flocks
Securely stray-a world within itself,
Disdaining all assault: there let me draw
Ethereal soul, there drink reviving gales
Profusely breathing from the spicy groves
And vales of fragrance, there at distance hear
The roaring floods and cataracts that sweep
From disembowelled earth the virgin gold,
And o'er the varied landscape restless rove,
Fervent with life of every fairer kind.
A land of wonders! which the sun still eyes
With ray direct, as of the lovely realm
Enamoured, and delighting there to dwell.

How changed the scene! In blazing height of noon,
The sun, oppressed, is plunged in thickest gloom.
Still horror reigns, a dreary twilight round,
Of struggling night and day malignant mixed.
For to the hot equator crowding fast,
Where, highly rarefied, the yielding air
Admits their stream, incessant vapours roll,
Amazing clouds on clouds continual heaped;
Or whirled tempestuous by the gusty wind,
Or silent borne along, heavy and slow,
With the big stores of steaming oceans charged.
Meantime, amid these upper seas, condensed
Around the cold aerial mountain's brow,
And by conflicting winds together dashed,
The Thunder holds his black tremendous throne;
From cloud to cloud the rending Lightnings rage;
Till, in the furious elemental war
Dissolved, the whole precipitated mass
Unbroken floods and solid torrents pours.

The treasures these, hid from the bounded search
Of ancient knowledge, whence with annual pomp,
Rich king of floods! o'erflows the swelling Nile.
From his two springs in Gojam's sunny realm
Pure-welling out, he through the lucid lake
Of fair Dambea rolls his infant stream.
There, by the Naiads nursed, he sports away
His playful youth amid the fragrant isles
That with unfading verdure smile around.
Ambitious thence the manly river breaks,
And, gathering many a flood, and copious fed

With all the mellowed treasures of the sky,
Winds in progressive majesty along:
Through splendid kingdoms now devolves his maze,
Now wanders wild o'er solitary tracts
Of life-deserted sand; till, glad to quit
The joyless desert, down the Nubian rocks
From thundering steep to steep he pours his urn,
And Egypt joys beneath the spreading wave.

His brother Niger too, and all the floods
In which the full-formed maids of Afric lave
Their jetty limbs, and all that from the tract
Of woody mountains stretched thro' gorgeous Ind
Fall on Cormandel's coast or Malabar;
From Menam's orient stream that nightly shines
With insect-lamps, to where Aurora sheds
On Indus' smiling banks the rosy shower—
All, at this bounteous season, ope their urns
And pour untoiling harvest o'er the land.

Nor less thy world, Columbus, drinks refreshed
The lavish moisture of the melting year.
Wide o'er his isles the branching Oronoque
Rolls a brown deluge, and the native drives
To dwell aloft on life-sufficing trees—
At once his dome, his robe, his food, and arms.
Swelled by a thousand streams, impetuous hurled
From all the roaring Andes, huge descends
The mighty Orellana. Scarce the muse
Dares stretch her wing o'er this enormous mass
Of rushing water; scarce she dares attempt
The sea-like Plata, to whose dread expanse,
Continuous depth, and wondrous length of course
Our floods are rills. With unabated force
In silent dignity they sweep along,
And traverse realms unknown, and blooming wilds,
And fruitful deserts-worlds of solitude
Where the sun smiles and seasons teem in vain,
Unseen and unenjoyed. Forsaking these,
O'er peopled plains they fair-diffusive flow
And many a nation feed, and circle safe
In their soft bosom many a happy isle,
The seat of blameless Pan, yet undisturbed
By Christian crimes and Europe's cruel sons.

Thus pouring on they proudly seek the deep,
Whose vanquish'd tide, recoiling from the shock,
Yields to this liquid weight of half the globe;

And Ocean trembles for his green domain.

But what avails this wondrous waste of wealth,
This gay profusion of luxurious bliss,
This pomp of Nature? what their balmy meads,
Their powerful herbs, and Ceres void of pain?
By vagrant birds dispersed and wafting winds,
What their unplanted fruits? What the cool draughts,
The ambrosial food, rich gums, and spicy health
Their forests yield? their toiling insects what,
Their silky pride and vegetable robes?
Ah! what avail their fatal treasures, hid
Deep in the bowels of the pitying earth,
Golconda's gems, and sad Potosi's mines
Where dwelt the gentlest children of the Sun?
What all that Afric's golden rivers roll,
Her odorous woods, and shining ivory stores?
Ill-fated race! the softening arts of peace,
Whate'er the humanizing muses teach,
The godlike wisdom of the tempered breast,
Progressive truth, the patient force of thought,
Investigation calm whose silent powers
Command the world, the light that leads to Heaven,
Kind equal rule, the government of laws,
And all-protecting freedom which alone
Sustains the name and dignity of man—
These are not theirs. The parent sun himself
Seems o'er this world of slaves to tyrannize,
And, with oppressive ray the roseate bloom
Of beauty blasting, gives the gloomy hue
And feature gross-or, worse, to ruthless deeds.
Mad jealousy, blind rage, and fell revenge
Their fervid spirit fires. Love dwells not there,
The soft regards, the tenderness of life,
The heart-shed tear, the ineffable delight
Of sweet humanity: these court the beam
Of milder climes-in selfish fierce desire
And the wild fury of voluptuous sense
There lost. The very brute creation there
This rage partakes, and burns with horrid fire.

Lo! the green serpent, from his dark abode,
Which even imagination fears to tread,
At noon forth-issuing, gathers up his train
In orbs immense, then, darting out anew,
Seeks the refreshing fount, by which diffused
He throws his folds; and while, with threatening tongue
And deathful jaws erect, the monster curls

His flaming crest, all other thirst appalled
Or shivering flies, or checked at distance stands,
Nor dares approach. But still more direful he,
The small close-lurking minister of fate,
Whose high-concocted venom through the veins
A rapid lightning darts, arresting swift
The vital current. Formed to humble man,
This child of vengeful Nature! There, sublimed
To fearless lust of blood, the savage race
Roam, licensed by the shading hour of guilt
And foul misdeed, when the pure day has shut
His sacred eye. The tiger, darting fierce
Impetuous on the prey his glance has doomed;
The lively-shining leopard, speckled o'er
With many a spot, the beauty of the waste;
And, scorning all the taming arts of man,
The keen hyena, fellest of the fell—
These, rushing from the inhospitable woods
Of Mauritania, or the tufted isles
That verdant rise amid the Libyan wild,
Innumerous glare around their shaggy king
Majestic stalking o'er the printed sand;
And with imperious and repeated roars
Demand their fated food. The fearful flocks
Crowd near the guardian swain; the nobler herds,
Where round their lordly bull in rural ease
They ruminating lie, with horror hear
The coming rage. The awakened village starts;
And to her fluttering breast the mother strains
Her thoughtless infant. From the pirate's den,
Or stern Morocco's tyrant fang escaped,
The wretch half wishes for his bonds again;
While, uproar all, the wilderness resounds
From Atlas eastward to the frighted Nile.

Unhappy he! who, from the first of joys,
Society, cut off, is left alone
Amid this world of death! Day after day,
Sad on the jutting eminence he sits,
And views the main that ever toils below;
Still fondly forming in the farthest verge,
Where the round ether mixes with the wave,
Ships, dim-discovered, dropping from the clouds;
At evening, to the setting sun he turns
A mournful eye, and down his dying heart
Sinks helpless; while the wonted roar is up,
And hiss continual through the tedious night.
Yet here, even here, into these black abodes

Of monsters, unappalled, from stooping Rome
And guilty Caesar, Liberty retired,
Her Cato following through Numidian wilds—
Disdainful of Campania's gentle plains
And all the green delights Ausonia pours,
When for them she must bend the servile knee,
And, fawning, take the splendid robber's boon.

Nor stop the terrors of these regions here.
Commissioned demons oft, angels of wrath,
Let loose the raging elements. Breathed hot
From all the boundless furnace of the sky,
And the wide glittering waste of burning sand,
A suffocating wind the pilgrim smites
With instant death. Patient of thirst and toil,
Son of the desert! even the camel feels,
Shot through his withered heart, the fiery blast.
Or from the black-red ether, bursting broad,
Sallies the sudden whirlwind. Straight the sands,
Commoved around, in gathering eddies play;
Nearer and nearer still they darkening come;
Till, with the general all-involving storm
Swept up, the whole continuous wilds arise;
And by their noon-day fount dejected thrown,
Or sunk at night in sad disastrous sleep,
Beneath descending hills the caravan
Is buried deep. In Cairo's crowded streets
The impatient merchant, wondering, waits in vain,
And Mecca saddens at the long delay.

But chief at sea, whose every flexile wave
Obeys the blast, the aerial tumult swells.
In the dread ocean, undulating wide,
Beneath the radiant line that girts the globe,
The circling typhon, whirled from point to point,
Exhausting all the rage of all the sky,
And dire ecnephia reign. Amid the heavens,
Falsely serene, deep in a cloudy speck
Compressed, the mighty tempest brooding dwells.
Of no regard, save to the skilful eye,
Fiery and foul, the small prognostic hangs
Aloft, or on the promontory's brow
Musters its force. A faint deceitful calm,
A fluttering gale, the demon sends before
To tempt the spreading sail. Then down at once
Precipitant descends a mingled mass
Of roaring winds and flame and rushing floods.
In wild amazement fixed the sailor stands.

Art is too slow. By rapid fate oppressed,
His broad-winged vessel drinks the whelming tide,
Hid in the bosom of the black abyss.
With such mad seas the daring Gama fought,
For many a day and many a dreadful night
Incessant labouring round the stormy Cape,
By bold ambition led, and bolder thirst
Of gold. For then from ancient gloom emerged
The rising world of trade: the genius then
Of navigation, that in hopeless sloth
Had slumbered on the vast Atlantic deep
For idle ages, starting, heard at last
The Lusitanian Prince, who, heaven-inspired,
To love of useful glory roused mankind,
And in unbounded commerce mixed the world.

Increasing still the terrors of these storms,
His jaws horrific armed with threefold fate,
Here dwells the direful shark. Lured by the scent
Of steaming crowds, of rank disease, and death,
Behold! he rushing cuts the briny flood,
Swift as the gale can bear the ship along;
And from the partners of that cruel trade
Which spoils unhappy Guinea of her sons
Demands his share of prey-demands themselves.
The stormy fates descend: one death involves
Tyrants and slaves; when straight, their mangled limbs
Crashing at once, he dyes the purple seas
With gore, and riots in the vengeful meal.

When o'er this world, by equinoctial rains
Flooded immense, looks out the joyless sun,
And draws the copious steam from swampy fens,
Where putrefaction into life ferments
And breathes destructive myriads, or from woods,
Impenetrable shades, recesses foul,
In vapours rank and blue corruption wrapt,
Whose gloomy horrors yet no desperate foot
Has ever dared to pierce; then wasteful forth
Walks the dire power of pestilent disease.
A thousand hideous fiends her course attend,
Sick nature blasting, and to heartless woe
And feeble desolation, casting down
The towering hopes and all the pride of man:
Such as of late at Carthagena quenched
The British fire. You, gallant Vernon, saw
The miserable scene; you, pitying, saw
To infant-weakness sunk the warrior's arm;

Saw the deep-racking pang, the ghastly form,
The lip pale-quivering, and the beamless eye
No more with ardour bright; you heard the groans
Of agonizing ships from shore to shore,
Heard, nightly plunged amid the sullen waves,
The frequent corse, while, on each other fixed
In sad presage, the blank assistants seemed
Silent to ask whom fate would next demand.

What need I mention those inclement skies
Where frequent o'er the sickening city, plague,
The fiercest child of Nemesis divine,
Descends? From Ethiopia's poisoned woods,
From stifled Cairo's filth, and fetid fields
With locust armies putrefying heaped,
This great destroyer sprung. Her awful rage
The brutes escape: Man is her destined prey,
Intemperate man! and o'er his guilty domes
She draws a close incumbent cloud of death;
Uninterrupted by the living winds,
Forbid to blow a wholesome breeze; and stained
With many a mixture by the Sun suffused
Of angry aspect. Princely wisdom then
Dejects his watchful eye; and from the hand
Of feeble justice ineffectual drop
The sword and balance; mute the voice of joy,
And hushed the clamour of the busy world.
Empty the streets, with uncouth verdure clad;
Into the worst of deserts sudden turned
The cheerful haunt of men-unless, escaped
From the doomed house, where matchless horror reigns,
Shut up by barbarous fear, the smitten wretch
With frenzy wild breaks loose, and, loud to Heaven
Screaming, the dreadful policy arraigns,
Inhuman and unwise. The sullen door,
Yet uninfected, on its cautious hinge
Fearing to turn, abhors society:
Dependents, friends, relations, Love himself,
Savaged by woe, forget the tender tie,
The sweet engagement of the feeling heart.
But vain their selfish care: the circling sky,
The wide enlivening air is full of fate;
And, struck by turns, in solitary pangs
They fall, unblest, untended, and unmourned.
Thus o'er the prostrate city black despair
Extends her raven wing; while, to complete
The scene of desolation stretched around,
The grim guards stand, denying all retreat,

And give the flying wretch a better death.

Much yet remains unsung: the rage intense
Of brazen-vaulted skies, of iron fields,
Where drought and famine starve the blasted year;
Fired by the torch of noon to tenfold rage,
The infuriate hill that shoots the pillared flame;
And, roused within the subterranean world,
The expanding earthquake, that resistless shakes
Aspiring cities from their solid base,
And buries mountains in the flaming gulf.
But 'tis enough; return, my vagrant muse;
A nearer scene of horror calls thee home.

Behold, slow-settling o'er the lurid grove
Unusual darkness broods, and growing, gains
The full possession of the sky, surcharged
With wrathful vapour, from the secret beds
Where sleep the mineral generations drawn.
Thence nitre, sulphur, and the fiery spume
Of fat bitumen, steaming on the day,
With various-tinctured trains of latent flame,
Pollute the sky, and in yon baleful cloud,
A reddening gloom, a magazine of fate,
Ferment; till, by the touch ethereal roused,
The dash of clouds, or irritating war
Of fighting winds, while all is calm below,
They furious spring. A boding silence reigns
Dread through the dun expanse-save the dull sound
That from the mountain, previous to the storm,
Rolls o'er the muttering earth, disturbs the flood,
And shakes the forest-leaf without a breath
Prone to the lowest vale the aerial tribes
Descend: the tempest-loving raven scarce
Dares wing the dubious dusk. In rueful gaze
The cattle stand, and on the scowling heavens
Cast a deploring eye-by man forsook,
Who to the crowded cottage hies him fast,
Or seeks the shelter of the downward cave.

'Tis listening fear and dumb amazement all:
When to the startled-eye the sudden glance
Appears far south, eruptive through the cloud,
And, following slower, in explosion vast
The thunder raises his tremendous voice.
At first, heard solemn o'er the verge of heaven,
The tempest growls; but as it nearer comes,
And rolls its awful burden on the wind,

The lightnings flash a larger curve, and more
The noise astounds, till overhead a sheet
Of livid flame discloses wide, then shuts
And opens wider, shuts and opens still
Expansive, wrapping ether in a blaze.
Follows the loosened aggravated roar,
Enlarging, deepening, mingling, peal on peal
Crushed horrible, convulsing heaven and earth.

Down comes a deluge of sonorous hail,
Or prone-descending rain. Wide-rent, the clouds
Pour a whole flood; and yet, its flame unquenched,
The unconquerable lightning struggles through,
Ragged and fierce, or in red whirling balls,
And fires the mountains with redoubled rage.
Black from the stroke, above, the smouldering pine
Stands a sad shattered trunk; and, stretched below,
A lifeless group the blasted cattle lie:
Here the soft flocks, with that same harmless look
They wore alive, and ruminating still
In fancy's eye; and there the frowning bull,
And ox half-raised. Struck on the castled cliff,
The venerable tower and spiry fane
Resign their aged pride. The gloomy woods
Start at the flash, and from their deep recess
Wide-flaming out, their trembling inmates shake.
Amid Carnarvon's mountains rages loud
The repercussive roar: with mighty crush,
Into the flashing deep, from the rude rocks
Of Penmanmaur heaped hideous to the sky,
Tumble the smitten cliffs; and Snowdon's peak,
Dissolving, instant yields his wintry load.
Far seen, the heights of heathy Cheviot blaze,
And Thule bellows through her utmost isles.

Guilt hears appalled, with deeply troubled thought;
And yet not always on the guilty head
Descends the fated flash. Young Celadon
And his Amelia were a matchless pair,
With equal virtue formed and equal grace
The same, distinguished by their sex alone:
Hers the mild lustre of the blooming morn,
And his the radiance of the risen day.

They loved: but such their guileless passion was
As in the dawn of time informed the heart
Of innocence and undissembling truth.
'Twas friendship heightened by the mutual wish,

The enchanting hope and sympathetic glow
Beamed from the mutual eye. Devoting all
To love, each was to each a dearer self,
Supremely happy in the awakened power
Of giving joy. Alone amid the shades,
Still in harmonious intercourse they lived
The rural day, and talked the flowing heart,
Or sighed and looked unutterable things.
So passed their life, a clear united stream,
By care unruffled; till, in evil hour,
The tempest caught them on the tender walk,
Heedless how far and where its mazes strayed,
While with each other blest, creative Love
Still bade eternal Eden smile around.
Heavy with instant fate, her bosom heaved
Unwonted sighs, and, stealing oft a look
Of the big gloom, on Celadon her eye
Fell tearful, wetting her disordered cheek.
In vain assuring love and confidence
In Heaven repressed her fear; it grew, and shook
Her frame near dissolution. He perceived
The unequal conflict, and, as angels look
On dying saints, his eyes compassion shed,
With love illumined high. 'Fear not,' he said,
'Sweet innocence! thou stranger to offence
And inward storm! he, who yon skies involves
In frowns of darkness, ever smiles on thee
With kind regard. O'er thee the secret shaft
That wastes at midnight, or the undreaded hour
Of noon, flies harmless: and that very voice,
Which thunders terror through the guilty heart,
With tongues of seraphs whispers peace to thine.
'Tis safety to be near thee sure, and thus
To clasp perfection!' From his void embrace,
Mysterious Heaven! that moment to the ground,
A blackened corse, was struck the beauteous maid.
But who can paint the lover, as he stood
Pierced by severe amazement, hating life,
Speechless, and fixed in all the death of woe?
So, faint resemblance! on the marble tomb
The well-dissembled mourner stooping stands,
For ever silent and for ever sad.

As from the face of Heaven the shattered clouds
Tumultuous rove, the interminable sky
Sublimer swells, and o'er the world expands
A purer azure. Nature from the storm
Shines out afresh; and through the lightened air

A higher lustre and a clearer calm
Diffusive tremble; while, as if in sign
Of danger past, a glittering robe of joy,
Set off abundant by the yellow ray,
Invests the fields, yet dropping from distress.

'Tis beauty all, and grateful song around,
Joined to the low of kine, and numerous bleat
Of flocks thick-nibbling through the clovered vale.
And shall the hymn be marred by thankless man,
Most-favoured, who with voice articulate
Should lead the chorus of this lower world?
Shall he, so soon forgetful of the hand
That hushed the thunder, and serenes the sky,
Extinguished feel that spark the tempest waked,
That sense of powers exceeding far his own,
Ere yet his feeble heart has lost its fears?

Cheered by the milder beam, the sprightly youth
Speeds to the well-known pool, whose crystal depth
A sandy bottom shows. Awhile he stands
Gazing the inverted landscape, half afraid
To meditate the blue profound below;
Then plunges headlong down the circling flood.
His ebon tresses and his rosy cheek
Instant emerge; and through the obedient wave,
At each short breathing by his lip repelled,
With arms and legs according well, he makes,
As humour leads, an easy-winding path;
While from his polished sides a dewy light
Effuses on the pleased spectators round.

This is the purest exercise of health,
The kind refresher of the summer heats;
Nor, when cold winter keens the brightening flood,
Would I weak-shivering linger on the brink.
Thus life redoubles, and is oft preserved
By the bold swimmer, in the swift illapse
Of accident disastrous. Hence the limbs
Knit into force; and the same Roman arm
That rose victorious o'er the conquered earth
First learned, while tender, to subdue the wave.
Even from the body's purity the mind
Receives a secret sympathetic aid.

Close in the covert of an hazel copse,
Where, winded into pleasing solitudes,
Runs out the rambling dale, young Damon sat

Pensive, and pierced with love's delightful pangs.
There to the stream that down the distant rocks
Hoarse-murmuring fell, and plaintive breeze that played
Among the bending willows, falsely he
Of Musidora's cruelty complained.
She felt his flame; but deep within her breast,
In bashful coyness or in maiden pride,
The soft return concealed; save when it stole
In side-long glances from her downcast eye,
Or from her swelling soul in stifled sighs.
Touched by the scene, no stranger to his vows,
He framed a melting lay to try her heart;
And, if an infant passion struggled there,
To call that passion forth. Thrice happy swain!
A lucky chance, that oft decides the fate
Of mighty monarchs, then decided thine!
For, lo! conducted by the laughing Loves,
This cool retreat his Musidora sought:
Warm in her cheek the sultry season glowed;
And, robed in loose array, she came to bathe
Her fervent limbs in the refreshing stream.
What shall he do? In sweet confusion lost,

'Twas then, beneath a secret waving shade
Where, winded into lovely solitudes,
Runs out the rambling dale, that Damon sat,
Thoughtful and fixed in philosophic muse.
And dubious flutterings, he a while remained.
A pure ingenuous elegance of soul,
A delicate refinement, known to few,
Perplexed his breast and urged him to retire:
But love forbade. Ye prudes in virtue, say,
Say, ye severest, what would you have done?
Meantime, this fairer nymph than ever blest
Arcadian stream, with timid eye around
The banks surveying, stripped her beauteous limbs
To taste the lucid coolness of the flood.
Ah! then, not Paris on the piny top
Of Ida panted stronger, when aside
The rival goddesses the veil divine
Cast unconfined, and gave him all their charms,
Than, Damon, thou; as from the snowy leg
And slender foot the inverted silk she drew;
As the soft touch dissolved the virgin zone;
And, through the parting robe, the alternate breast,
With youth wild-throbbing, on thy lawless gaze
In full luxuriance rose. But, desperate youth,
How durst thou risk the soul-distracting view

As from her naked limbs of glowing white,
Harmonious swelled by nature's finest hand,
In folds loose-floating fell the fainter lawn,
And fair exposed she stood, shrunk from herself,
With fancy blushing, at the doubtful breeze
Alarmed, and starting like the fearful fawn?
Then to the flood she rushed: the parted flood
Its lovely guest with closing waves received;
And every beauty softening, every grace
Flushing anew, a mellow lustre shed—
As shines the lily through the crystal mild,
Or as the rose amid the morning dew,
Fresh from Aurora's hand, more sweetly glows.
While thus she wantoned, now beneath the wave
But ill-concealed, and now with streaming locks,
That half-embraced her in a humid veil,
Rising again, the latent Damon drew
Such maddening draughts of beauty to the soul
As for a while o'erwhelmed his raptured thought
With luxury too daring. Checked, at last,
By love's respectful modesty, he deemed
The theft profane, if aught profane to love
Can e'er be deemed, and, struggling from the shade,
With headlong hurry fled: but first these lines,
Traced by his ready pencil, on the bank
With trembling hand he threw-'Bathe on, my fair,
Yet unbeheld save by the sacred eye
Of faithful love: I go to guard thy haunt;
To keep from thy recess each vagrant foot
And each licentious eye.' With wild surprise,
As if to marble struck, devoid of sense,
A stupid moment motionless she stood:
So stands the statue that enchants the world;
So, bending, tries to veil the matchless boast,
The mingled beauties of exulting Greece.
Recovering, swift she flew to find those robes
Which blissful Eden knew not; and, arrayed
In careless haste, the alarming paper snatched.
But, when her Damon's well-known hand she saw,
Her terrors vanished, and a softer train
Or mixed emotions, hard to be described,
Her sudden bosom seized: shame void of guilt,
The charming blush of innocence, esteem
And admiration of her lover's flame,
By modesty exalted, even a sense
Of self-approving beauty stole across
Her busy thought. At length, a tender calm
Hushed by degrees the tumult of her soul;

And on the spreading beech, that o'er the stream
Incumbent hung, she with the sylvan pen
Of rural lovers this confession carved,
Which soon her Damon kissed with weeping joy:
'Dear youth! sole judge of what these verses mean,
By fortune too much favoured, but by love,
Alas! not favoured less, be still as now
Discreet: the time may come you need not fly.'

The Sun has lost his rage: his downward orb
Shoots nothing now but animating warmth
And vital lustre; that with various ray,
Lights up the clouds, those beauteous robes of heaven,
Incessant rolled into romantic shapes,
The dream of waking fancy! Broad below,
Covered with ripening fruits, and swelling fast
Into the perfect year, the pregnant earth
And all her tribes rejoice. Now the soft hour
Of walking comes for him who lonely loves
To seek the distant hills, and there converse
With nature, there to harmonize his heart,
And in pathetic song to breathe around
The harmony to others. Social friends,
Attuned to happy unison of soul—
To whose exulting eye a fairer world,
Of which the vulgar never had a glimpse,
Displays its charms; whose minds are richly fraught
With philosophic stores, superior light;
And in whose breast enthusiastic burns
Virtue, the sons of interest deem romance—
Now called abroad, enjoy the falling day:
Now to the verdant portico of woods,
To nature's vast Lyceum, forth they walk;
By that kind school where no proud master reigns,
The full free converse of the friendly heart,
Improving and improved. Now from the world,
Sacred to sweet retirement, lovers steal,
And pour their souls in transport, which the sire
Of love approving hears, and calls it good.
Which way, Amanda, shall we bend our course?
The choice perplexes. Wherefore should we choose?
All is the same with thee. Say, shall we wind
Along the streams? or walk the smiling mead?
Or court the forest glades? or wander wild
Among the waving harvests? or ascend,
While radiant Summer opens all its pride,
Thy hill, delightful Shene? Here let us sweep
The boundless landscape; now the raptured eye,

Exulting swift, to huge Augusta send,
Now to the sister hills that skirt her plain,
To lofty Harrow now, and now to where
Majestic Windsor lifts his princely brow.
In lovely contrast to this glorious view,
Calmly magnificent, then will we turn
To where the silver Thames first rural grows.
There let the feasted eye unwearied stray;
Luxurious, there, rove through the pendent woods
That nodding hang o'er Harrington's retreat;
And, stooping thence to Ham's embowering walks,
Beneath whose shades, in spotless peace retired,
With her the pleasing partner of his heart,
The worthy Queensberry yet laments his Gay,
And polished Cornbury woos the willing muse,
Slow let us trace the matchless vale of Thames;
Fair-winding up to where the muses haunt
In Twit'nam's bowers, and for their Pope implore
The healing god; to royal Hampton's pile,
To Clermont's terraced height, and Esher's groves,
Where in the sweetest solitude, embraced
By the soft windings of the silent Mole,
From courts and senates Pelham finds repose.
Enchanting vale! beyond whate'er the muse
Has of Achaia or Hesperia sung!
O vale of bliss! O softly-swelling hills!
On which the power of cultivation lies,
And joys to see the wonders of his toil.

Heavens! what a goodly prospect spreads around,
Of hills, and dales, and woods, and lawns, and spires,
And glittering towns, and gilded streams, till all
The stretching landskip into smoke decays!
Happy Britannia! where the Queen of Arts,
Inspiring vigour, Liberty, abroad
Walks unconfined even to thy farthest cots,
And scatters plenty with unsparing hand.

Rich is thy soil, and merciful thy clime;
Thy streams unfailing in the Summer's drought;
Unmatched thy guardian-oaks; thy valleys float
With golden waves; and on thy mountains flocks
Bleat numberless; while, roving round their sides,
Bellow the blackening herds in lusty droves.
Beneath, thy meadows glow, and rise unquelled
Against the mower's scythe. On every hand
Thy villas shine. Thy country teems with wealth;
And Property assures it to the swain,

Pleased and unwearied in his guarded toil.

Full are thy cities with the sons of art;
And trade and joy, in every busy street,
Mingling are heard: even Drudgery himself,
As at the car he sweats, or, dusty, hews
The palace stone, looks gay. Thy crowded ports,
Where rising masts an endless prospect yield,
With labour burn, and echo to the shouts
Of hurried sailor, as he hearty waves
His last adieu, and, loosening every sheet,
Resigns the spreading vessel to the wind.

Bold, firm, and graceful, are thy generous youth,
By hardship sinewed, and by danger fired,
Scattering the nations where they go; and first
Or in the listed plain or stormy seas.
Thy sons of glory many! Alfred thine,
In whom the splendour of heroic war,
And more heroic peace, when governed well,
Combine; whose hallowed name the Virtues saint,
And his own muses love; the best of kings!
With him thy Edwards and thy Henrys shine,
Names dear to fame; the first who deep impressed
On haughty Gaul the terror of thy arms,
That awes her genius still. In statesmen thou,
And patriots, fertile. Thine a steady More,
Who, with a generous though mistaken zeal,
Withstood a brutal tyrant's useful rage;
Like Cato firm, like Aristides just,
Like rigid Cincinnatus nobly poor—
A dauntless soul erect, who smil'd on death.
Frugal and wise, a Walsingham is thine;
A Drake, who made thee mistress of the deep,
And bore thy name in thunder round the world.
Then flamed thy spirit high. But who can speak
The numerous worthies of the maiden reign?
In Raleigh mark their every glory mixed—
Raleigh, the scourge of Spain! whose breast with all
The sage, the patriot, and the hero burned.
Nor sunk his vigour when a coward reign
The warrior fettered, and at last resigned,
To glut the vengeance of a vanquished foe.
Then, active still and unrestrained, his mind
Explored the vast extent of ages past,
And with his prison-hours enriched the world;
Yet found no times, in all the long research,
So glorious, or so base, as those he proved,

In which he conquered, and in which he bled.
Nor can the muse the gallant Sidney pass,
The plume of war! with early laurels crowned,
The lover's myrtle and the poet's bay.
A Hampden too is thine, illustrious land!
Wise, strenuous, firm, of unsubmitting soul,
Who stemmed the torrent of a downward age
To slavery prone, and bade thee rise again,
In all thy native pomp of freedom bold.
Bright at his call thy age of men effulged;
Of men on whom late time a kindling eye
Shall turn, and tyrants tremble while they read.
Bring every sweetest flower, and let me strew
The grave where Russel lies, whose tempered blood,
With calmest cheerfulness for thee resigned,
Stained the sad annals of a giddy reign
Aiming at lawless power, though meanly sunk
In loose inglorious luxury. With him
His friend, the British Cassius, fearless bled;
Of high determined spirit, roughly brave,
By ancient learning to the enlighten'd love
Of ancient freedom warmed. Fair thy renown
In awful sages and in noble bards;
Soon as the light of dawning Science spread
Her orient ray, and waked the Muses' song.
Thine is a Bacon, hapless in his choice,
Unfit to stand the civil storm of state,
And, through the smooth barbarity of courts,
With firm but pliant virtue forward still
To urge his course: him for the studious shade
Kind Nature formed, deep, comprehensive, clear,

Exact, and elegant; in one rich soul,
Plato, the Stagyrite, and Tully joined.
The great deliverer he, who, from the gloom
Of cloistered monks and jargon-teaching schools,
Led forth the true philosophy, there long
Held in the magic chain of words and forms
And definitions void: he led her forth,
Daughter of Heaven! that, slow-ascending still,
Investigating sure the chain of things,
With radiant finger points to Heaven again.
The generous Ashley thine, the friend of man,
Who scanned his nature with a brother's eye,
His weakness prompt to shade, to raise his aim,
To touch the finer movements of the mind,
And with the moral beauty charm the heart.

Why need I name thy Boyle, whose pious search,
Amid the dark recesses of his works,
The great Creator sought? And why thy Locke,
Who made the whole internal world his own?
Let Newton, pure intelligence, whom God
To mortals lent to trace his boundless works
From laws sublimely simple, speak thy fame
In all philosophy. For lofty sense,
Creative fancy, and inspection keen
Through the deep windings of the human heart,
Is not wild Shakespeare thine and nature's boast?
Is not each great, each amiable muse
Of classic ages in thy Milton met?
A genius universal as his theme,
Astonishing as chaos, as the bloom
Of blowing Eden fair, as heaven sublime!
Nor shall my verse that elder bard forget,
The gentle Spenser, fancy's pleasing son;
Who, like a copious river, poured his song
O'er all the mazes of enchanted ground;
Nor thee, his ancient master, laughing sage,
Chaucer, whose native manners-painting verse,
Well moralized, shines through the Gothic cloud
Of time and language o'er thy genius thrown.

May my song soften as thy daughters I,
Britannia, hail! for beauty is their own,
The feeling heart, simplicity of life,
And elegance, and taste; the faultless form,
Shaped by the hand of harmony; the cheek,
Where the live crimson, through the native white
Soft-shooting, o'er the face diffuses bloom
And every nameless grace; the parted lip,
Like the red rosebud moist with morning dew,
Breathing delight; and, under flowing jet,
Or sunny ringlets, or of circling brown,
The neck slight-shaded and the swelling breast;
The look resistless, piercing to the soul,
And by the soul informed, when, dressed in love,
She sits high-smiling in the conscious eye.

Island of bliss! amid the subject seas
That thunder round thy rocky coasts, set up,
At once the wonder, terror, and delight,
Of distant nations, whose remotest shore
Can soon be shaken by thy naval arm;
Not to be shook thyself, but all assaults
Baffling, like thy hoar cliffs the loud sea-wave.

O Thou, by whose almighty nod the scale
Of empire rises, or alternate falls,
Send forth the saving Virtues round the land
In bright patrol-white Peace, and social Love;
The tender-looking Charity, intent
On gentle deeds, and shedding tears through smiles;
Undaunted Truth, and Dignity of mind;
Courage, composed and keen; sound Temperance,
Healthful in heart and look; clear Chastity,
With blushes reddening as she moves along,
Disordered at the deep regard she draws;
Rough Industry; Activity untired,
With copious life informed, and all awake:
While in the radiant front superior shines
That first paternal virtue, Public Zeal,
Who throws o'er all an equal, wide survey,
And, ever musing on the common weal,
Still labours glorious with some great design.

Low walks the sun, and broadens by degrees,
Just o'er the verge of day. The shifting clouds
Assembled gay, a richly-gorgeous train,
In all their pomp attend his setting throne.
Air, earth, and ocean smile immense. And now,
As if his weary chariot sought the bowers
Of Amphitrite and her tending nymphs,
(So Grecian fable sung) he dips his orb;
Now half-immersed; and now, a golden curve,
Gives one bright glance, then total disappears.

For ever running an enchanted round,
Passes the day, deceitful, vain, and void;
As fleets the vision o'er the formful brain,
This moment hurrying wild the impassioned soul,
The next in nothing lost. 'Tis so to him,
The dreamer of this earth, an idle blank—
A sight of horror to the cruel wretch,
Who, all day long in sordid pleasure rolled,
Himself an useless load, has squandered vile
Upon his scoundrel train what might have cheered
A drooping family of modest worth.
But to the generous, still-improving mind
That gives the hopeless heart to sing for joy,
Diffusing kind beneficence around
Boastless as now descends the silent dew—
To him the long review of ordered life
Is inward rapture only to be felt.

Confessed from yonder slow-extinguished clouds,
All ether softening, sober Evening takes
Her wonted station in the middle air,
A thousand shadows at her beck. First this
She sends on earth; then that of deeper dye
Steals soft behind; and then a deeper still,
In circle following circle, gathers round
To close the face of things. A fresher gale
Begins to wave the wood and stir the stream,
Sweeping with shadowy gust the fields of corn,
While the quail clamours for his running mate.
Wide o'er the thistly lawn, as swells the breeze,
A whitening shower of vegetable down
Amusive floats. The kind impartial care
Of Nature naught disdains: thoughtful to feed
Her lowest sons, and clothe the coming year,
From field to field the feathered seeds she wings.

His folded flock secure, the shepherd home
Hies, merry-hearted; and by turns relieves
The ruddy milk-maid of her brimming pail—
The beauty whom perhaps his witless heart,
Unknowing what the joy-mixed anguish means,
Sincerely loves, by that best language shown
Of cordial glances and obliging deeds.

Onward they pass, o'er many a panting height
And valley sunk and unfrequented; where
At fall of eve the fairy people throng,
In various game and revelry to pass
The summer night, as village stories tell.
But far about they wander from the grave
Of him whom his ungentle fortune urged
Against his own sad breast to lift the hand
Of impious violence. The lonely tower
Is also shunned; whose mournful chambers hold,
So night-struck fancy dreams, the yelling ghost.

Among the crooked lanes, on every hedge,
The Glow-worm lights his gem; and, through the dark,
A moving radiance twinkles. Evening yields
The world to Night; not in her winter robe
Of massy Stygian woof, but loose arrayed
In mantle dun. A faint erroneous ray,
Glanced from the imperfect surfaces of things,
Flings half an image on the straining eye;
While wavering woods, and villages, and streams,

And rocks, and mountain-tops that long retained
The ascending gleam are all one swimming scene,
Uncertain if beheld. Sudden to heaven
Thence weary vision turns; where, leading soft
The silent hours of love, with purest ray
Sweet Venus shines; and, from her genial rise,
When daylight sickens, till it springs afresh,
Unrivalled reigns, the fairest lamp of night.
As thus the effulgence tremulous I drink,
With cherished gaze, the lambent lightnings shoot
Across the sky, or horizontal dart
In wondrous shapes-by fearful murmuring crowds
Portentous deemed. Amid the radiant orbs
That more than deck, that animate the sky,
The life-infusing suns of other worlds,
Lo! from the dread immensity of space
Returning with accelerated course,
The rushing comet to the sun descends;
And, as he sinks below the shading earth,
With awful train projected o'er the heavens,
The guilty nations tremble. But, above
Those superstitious horrors that enslave
The fond sequacious herd, to mystic faith
And blind amazement prone, the enlightened few,
Whose godlike minds philosophy exalts,
The glorious stranger hail. They feel a joy
Divinely great; they in their powers exult,
That wondrous force of thought, which mounting spurns
This dusky spot, and measures all the sky;
While, from his far excursions through the wilds
Of barren ether, faithful to his time,
They see the blazing wonder rise anew,
In seeming terror clad, but kindly bent
To work the will of all-sustaining love—
From his huge vapoury train perhaps to shake
Reviving moisture on the numerous orbs
Through which his long ellipsis winds, perhaps
To lend new fuel to declining suns,
To light up worlds, and feed the eternal fire.

With thee, serene Philosophy, with thee,
And thy bright garland, let me crown my song!
Effusive source of evidence and truth!
A lustre shedding o'er the ennobled mind,
Stronger than summer-noon, and pure as that
Whose mild vibrations soothe the parted soul,
New to the dawning of celestial day.
Hence through her nourished powers, enlarged by thee,

She springs aloft, with elevated pride,
Above the tangling mass of low desires,
That bind the fluttering crowd; and, angel-winged,
The heights of science and of virtue gains,
Where all is calm and clear; with Nature round,
Or in the starry regions or the abyss,
To reason's and to fancy's eye displayed—
The first up-tracing, from the dreary void,
The chain of causes and effects to Him,
The world-producing Essence, who alone
Possesses being; while the last receives
The whole magnificence of heaven and earth,
And every beauty, delicate or bold,
Obvious or more remote, with livelier sense,
Diffusive painted on the rapid mind.

Tutored by thee, hence Poetry exalts
Her voice to ages; and informs the page
With music, image, sentiment, and thought,
Never to die; the treasure of mankind,
Their highest honour, and their truest joy!

Without thee what were unenlightened man?
A savage, roaming through the woods and wilds
In quest of prey; and with the unfashioned fur
Rough-clad; devoid of every finer art
And elegance of life. Nor happiness
Domestic, mixed of tenderness and care,
Nor moral excellence, nor social bliss,
Nor guardian law were his; nor various skill
To turn the furrow, or to guide the tool
Mechanic; nor the heaven-conducted prow
Of Navigation bold, that fearless braves
The burning line or dares the wintry pole,
Mother severe of infinite delights!
Nothing, save rapine, indolence, and guile,
And woes on woes, a still-revolving train!
Whose horrid circle had made human life
Than non-existence worse: but, taught by thee,
Ours are the plans of policy and peace;
To live like brothers, and, conjunctive all,
Embellish life. While thus laborious crowds
Ply the tough oar, Philosophy directs
The ruling helm; or, like the liberal breath
Of potent heaven, invisible, the sail
Swells out, and bears the inferior world along.

Nor to this evanescent speck of earth

Poorly confined: the radiant tracts on high
Are her exalted range; intent to gaze
Creation through; and, from that full complex
Of never-ending wonders, to conceive
Of the Sole Being right, who spoke the word,
And Nature moved complete. With inward view,
Thence on the ideal kingdom swift she turns
Her eye; and instant, at her powerful glance,
The obedient phantoms vanish or appear;
Compound, divide, and into order shift,
Each to his rank, from plain perception up
To the fair forms of fancy's fleeting train;
To reason then, deducing truth from truth,
And notion quite abstract; where first begins
The world of spirits, action all, and life
Unfettered and unmixed. But here the cloud,
So wills Eternal Providence, sits deep.
Enough for us to know that this dark state,
In wayward passions lost and vain pursuits,
This infancy of being, cannot prove
The final issue of the works of God,
By boundless love and perfect wisdom formed,
And ever rising with the rising mind.

AUTUMN

THE ARGUMENT

The subject proposed. Addressed to Mr. Onslow. A prospect of the fields ready for harvest. Reflections in praise of industry raised by that view. Reaping. A tale relative to it. A harvest storm. Shooting and hunting; their barbarity. A ludicrous account of foxhunting. A view of an orchard. Wall fruit. A vineyard. A description of fogs, frequent in the latter part of Autumn; whence a digression, inquiring into the rise of fountains and rivers. Birds of season considered, that now shift their habitation. The prodigious number of them that cover the northern and western isles of Scotland. Hence a view of the country. A prospect of the discoloured, fading woods. After a gentle dusky day, moonlight. Autumnal meteors. Morning; to which succeeds a calm, pure, sunshiny day, such as usually shuts up the season. The harvest being gathered in, the country dissolved in joy. The whole concludes with a panegyric on a philosophical country life.

Crowned with the sickle and the wheaten sheaf
While Autumn nodding o'er the yellow plain
Comes jovial on, the Doric reed once more
Well-pleased I tune. Whate'er the Wintry frost
Nitrous prepared, the various-blossomed Spring
Put in white promise forth, and Summer-suns

Concocted strong, rush boundless now to view,
Full, perfect all, and swell my glorious theme.

Onslow! the muse, ambitious of thy name
To grace, inspire, and dignify her song,
Would from the public voice thy gentle ear
A while engage. Thy noble cares she knows,
The patriot-virtues that distend thy thought,
Spread on thy front, and in thy bosom glow;
While listening senates hang upon thy tongue,
Devolving through the maze of eloquence
A roll of periods, sweeter than her song.
But she too pants for public virtue; she,
Though weak of power, yet strong in ardent will,
Whene'er her country rushes on her heart,
Assumes a bolder note, and fondly tries
To mix the patriot's with the poet's flame.

When the bright Virgin gives the beauteous days,
And Libra weighs in equal scales the year,
From heaven's high cope the fierce effulgence shook
Of parting Summer, a serener blue,
With golden light enlivened, wide invests
The happy world. Attempered suns arise
Sweet-beamed, and shedding oft through lucid clouds
A pleasing calm; while broad and brown, below,
Extensive harvests hang the heavy head.
Rich, silent, deep they stand; for not a gale
Rolls its light billows o'er the bending plain;
A calm of plenty! till the ruffled air
Falls from its poise, and gives the breeze to blow.
Rent is the fleecy mantle of the sky;
The clouds fly different; and the sudden sun
By fits effulgent gilds the illumined field,
And black by fits the shadows sweep along—
A gaily chequered, heart-expanding view,
Far as the circling eye can shoot around,
Unbounded tossing in a flood of corn.
These are thy blessings, Industry, rough power!
Whom labour still attends, and sweat, and pain;
Yet the kind source of every gentle art
And all the soft civility of life:
Raiser of human kind! by nature cast
Naked and helpless out amid the woods
And wilds to rude inclement elements;
With various seeds of art deep in the mind
Implanted, and profusely poured around
Materials infinite; but idle all,

Still unexerted, in the unconscious breast
Slept the lethargic powers; Corruption still
Voracious swallowed what the liberal hand
Of Bounty scattered o'er the savage year.
And still the sad barbarian roving mixed
With beasts of prey; or for his acorn meal
Fought the fierce tusky boar—a shivering wretch!
Aghast and comfortless when the bleak north,
With winter charged, let the mixed tempest fly,
Hail, rain, and snow, and bitter-breathing frost.
Then to the shelter of the hut he fled,
And the wild season, sordid, pined away;
For home he had not: home is the resort
Of love, of joy, of peace and plenty, where,
Supporting and supported, polished friends
And dear relations mingle into bliss.
But this the rugged savage never felt,
Even desolate in crowds; and thus his days
Rolled heavy, dark, and unenjoyed along—
A waste of time! till Industry approached,
And roused him from his miserable sloth;
His faculties unfolded; pointed out
Where lavish Nature the directing hand
Of Art demanded; showed him how to raise
His feeble force by the mechanic powers,
To dig the mineral from the vaulted earth,
On what to turn the piercing rage of fire,
On what the torrent, and the gathered blast;
Gave the tall ancient forest to his axe;
Taught him to chip the wood, and hew the stone,
Till by degrees the finished fabric rose;
Tore from his limbs the blood-polluted fur,
And wrapt them in the woolly vestment warm,
Or bright in glossy silk, and flowing lawn;
With wholesome viands filled his table, poured
The generous glass around, inspired to wake
The life-refining soul of decent wit;
Nor stopped at barren bare necessity;
But, still advancing bolder, led him on
To pomp, to pleasure, elegance, and grace;
And, breathing high ambition through his soul,
Set science, wisdom, glory in his view,
And bade him be the lord of all below.
Then gathering men their natural powers combined,
And formed a public; to the general good
Submitting, aiming, and conducting all.
For this the patriot-council met, the full,
The free, and fairly represented whole;

For this they planned the holy guardian laws,
Distinguished orders, animated arts,
And, with joint force Oppression chaining, set
Imperial Justice at the helm, yet still
To them accountable: nor slavish dreamed
That toiling millions must resign their weal
And all the honey of their search to such
As for themselves alone themselves have raised.

Hence every form of cultivated life
In order set, protected, and inspired
Into perfection wrought. Uniting all,
Society grew numerous, high, polite,
And happy. Nurse of art, the city reared
In beauteous pride her tower-encircled head;
And, stretching street on street, by thousands drew,
From twining woody haunts, or the tough yew
To bows strong-straining, her aspiring sons.

Then commerce brought into the public walk
The busy merchant; the big warehouse built;
Raised the strong crane; choked up the loaded street
With foreign plenty; and thy stream, O Thames,
Large, gentle, deep, majestic, king of floods!
Chose for his grand resort. On either hand,
Like a long wintry forest, groves of masts
Shot up their spires; the bellying sheet between
Possessed the breezy void; the sooty hulk
Steered sluggish on; the splendid barge along
Rowed regular to harmony; around,
The boat light-skimming stretched its oary wings;
While deep the various voice of fervent toil
From bank to bank increased; whence, ribbed with oak
To bear the British thunder, black, and bold,
The roaring vessel rushed into the main.

Then too the pillared dome magnific heaved
Its ample roof; and luxury within
Poured out her glittering stores. The canvas smooth,
With glowing life protuberant, to the view
Embodied rose; the statue seemed to breathe
And soften into flesh beneath the touch
Of forming art, imagination-flushed.

All is the gift of industry-whate'er
Exalts, embellishes, and renders life
Delightful. Pensive Winter, cheered by him,
Sits at the social fire, and happy hears

The excluded tempest idly rave along;
His hardened fingers deck the gaudy Spring;
Without him Summer were an arid waste;
Nor to the Autumnal months could thus transmit
Those full, mature, immeasurable stores
That, waving round, recall my wandering song.

Soon as the morning trembles o'er the sky,
And unperceived unfolds the spreading day,
Before the ripened field the reapers stand
In fair array, each by the lass he loves,
To bear the rougher part and mitigate
By nameless gentle offices her toil.
At once they stoop, and swell the lusty sheaves;
While through their cheerful band the rural talk,
The rural scandal, and the rural jest
Fly harmless, to deceive the tedious time
And steal unfelt the sultry hours away.
Behind the master walks, builds up the shocks,
And, conscious, glancing oft on every side
His sated eye, feels his heart heave with joy.
The gleaners spread around, and here and there,
Spike after spike, their sparing harvest pick.
Be not too narrow, husbandmen! but fling
From the full sheaf with charitable stealth
The liberal handful. Think, oh! grateful think
How good the God of harvest is to you,
Who pours abundance o'er your flowing fields,
While these unhappy partners of your kind
Wide-hover round you, like the fowls of heaven,
And ask their humble dole. The various turns
Of fortune ponder; that your sons may want
What now with hard reluctance faint ye give.

The lovely young Lavinia once had friends;
And fortune smiled deceitful on her birth.
For, in her helpless years deprived of all,
Of every stay save innocence and Heaven,
She, with her widowed mother, feeble, old,
And poor, lived in a cottage far retired
Among the windings of a woody vale;
By solitude and deep surrounding shades,
But more by bashful modesty, concealed.
Together thus they shunned the cruel scorn
Which virtue, sunk to poverty, would meet
From giddy fashion and low-minded pride;
Almost on nature's common bounty fed,
Like the gay birds that sung them to repose,

Content, and careless of to-morrow's fare.
Her form was fresher than the morning-rose
When the dew wets its leaves; unstained and pure
As is the lily or the mountain-snow.
The modest virtues mingled in her eyes,
Still on the ground dejected, darting all
Their humid beams into the blooming flowers:
Or when the mournful tale her mother told,
Of what her faithless fortune promised once,
Thrilled in her thought, they, like the dewy star
Of evening, shone in tears. A native grace
Sat fair-proportioned on her polished limbs,
Veiled in a simple robe, their best attire,
Beyond the pomp of dress; for loveliness
Needs not the foreign aid of ornament,
But is when unadorned adorned the most.
Thoughtless of beauty, she was beauty's self,
Recluse amid the close-embowering woods.

As in the hollow breast of Apennine,
Beneath the shelter of encircling hills,
A myrtle rises, far from human eye,
And breathes its balmy fragrance o'er the wild—
So flourished blooming, and unseen by all,
The sweet Lavinia; till at length, compelled
By strong necessity's supreme command,
With smiling patience in her looks she went
To glean Palemon's fields. The pride of swains
Palemon was, the generous and the rich,
Who led the rural life in all its joy
And elegance, such as Arcadian song
Transmits from ancient uncorrupted times,
When tyrant custom had not shackled man,
But free to follow nature was the mode.
He then, his fancy with autumnal scenes
Amusing, chanced beside his reaper-train
To walk, when poor Lavinia drew his eye;
Unconscious of her power, and turning quick
With unaffected blushes from his gaze—
He saw her charming, but he saw not half
The charms her downcast modesty concealed.
That very moment love and chaste desire
Sprung in his bosom, to himself unknown;
For still the world prevailed, and its dread laugh,
Which scarce the firm philosopher can scorn,
Should his heart own a gleaner in the field;
And thus in secret to his soul he sighed:
'What pity that so delicate a form,

By beauty kindled, where enlivening sense
And more than vulgar goodness seem to dwell,
Should be devoted to the rude embrace
Of some indecent clown! She looks, methinks,
Of old Acasto's line; and to my mind
Recalls that patron of my happy life,
From whom my liberal fortune took its rise,
Now to the dust gone down, his houses, lands,
And once fair-spreading family dissolved.
'Tis said that in some lone, obscure retreat,
Urged by remembrance sad and decent pride,
Far from those scenes which knew their better days,
His aged widow and his daughter live;
Whom yet my fruitless search could never find.
Romantic wish, would this the daughter were!'

When, strict inquiring, from herself he found
She was the same, the daughter of his friend,
Of bountiful Acasto, who can speak
The mingled passions that surprised his heart
And through his nerves in shivering transport ran?
Then blazed his smothered flame, avowed and bold
And, as he viewed her ardent o'er and o'er,
Love, gratitude, and pity wept at once.
Confused and frightened at his sudden tears,
Her rising beauties flushed a higher bloom,
As thus Palemon, passionate and just,
Poured out the pious rapture of his soul:
'And art thouu then Acasto's dear remains?
She whom my restless gratitude has sought
So long in vain? O yes! the very same,
The softened image of my noble friend,
Alive his every feature, every look,
More elegantly touched. Sweeter than Spring!
Thou sole surviving blossom from the root
That nourished up my fortune! say, ah where,
In what sequestered desert, hast thou drawn
The kindest aspect of delighted Heaven?
Into such beauty spread, and blown so fair?
Though poverty's cold wind and crushing rain
Beat keen and heavy on thy tender years.
Oh, let me now into a richer soil
Transplant thee safe, where vernal suns and showers
Diffuse their warmest, largest influence;
And of my garden be the pride and joy!
It ill befits thee, oh, it ill befits
Acasto's daughter-his, whose open stores,
Though vast, were little to his ampler heart,

The father of a country-thus to pick
The very refuse of those harvest-fields
Which from his bounteous friendship I enjoy.
Then throw that shameful pittance from thy hand,
But ill applied to such a rugged task;
The fields, the master, all, my fair, are thine;
If, to the various blessings which thy house
Has on me lavish'd, thou wilt add that bliss,
That dearest bliss, the power of blessing thee!'

Here ceased the youth: yet still his speaking eye
Expressed the sacred triumph of his soul,
With conscious virtue, gratitude, and love
Above the vulgar joy divinely raised.
Nor waited he reply. Won by the charm
Of goodness irresistible, and all
In sweet disorder lost, she blushed consent.
The news immediate to her mother brought,
While, pierced with anxious thought, she pined away
The lonely moments for Lavinia's fate,
Amazed, and scarce believing what she heard,
Joy seized her wither'd veins, and one bright gleam
Of setting life shone on her evening hours,
Not less enraptured than the happy pair;
Who flourished long in tender bliss, and reared
A numerous offspring, lovely like themselves,
And good, the grace of all the country round.

Defeating oft the labours of the year,
The sultry south collects a potent blast.
At first, the groves are scarcely seen to stir
Their trembling tops; and a still murmur runs
Along the soft-inclining fields of corn.
But, as the aerial tempest fuller swells,
And in one mighty stream, invisible,
Immense, the whole excited atmosphere
Impetuous rushes o'er the sounding world—
Strained to the root, the stooping forest pours
A rustling shower of yet untimely leaves.
High-beat, the circling mountains eddy in,
From the bare wild, the dissipated storm,
And send it in a torrent down the vale.
Exposed, and naked to its utmost rage,
Through all the sea of harvest rolling round,
The billowy plain floats wide; nor can evade,
Though pliant to the blast, its seizing force—
Or whirled in air or into vacant chaff
Shook waste. And sometimes too a burst of rain,

Swept from the black horizon, broad descends
In one continuous flood. Still over head
The mingling tempest weaves its gloom, and still
The deluge deepens; till the fields around
Lie sunk and flatted in the sordid wave.
Sudden the ditches swell; the meadows swim.
Red from the hills innumerable streams
Tumultuous roar, and high above its banks
The river lift-before whose rushing tide
Herds, flocks, and harvests, cottages, and swains
Roll mingled down; all that the winds had spared
In one wild moment ruined, the big hopes
And well-earned treasures of the painful year.
Fled to some eminence, the husbandman
Helpless beholds the miserable wreck
Driving along; his drowning ox, at once
Descending with his labours scattered round,
He sees; and instant o'er his shivering thought
Comes winter unprovided, and a train
Of clamant children dear. Ye masters, then
Be mindful of the rough laborious hand
That sinks you soft in elegance and ease;
Be mindful of those limbs in russet clad
Whose toil to yours is warmth and graceful pride;
And oh, be mindful of that sparing board
Which covers yours with luxury profuse,
Makes your glass sparkle, and your sense rejoice;
Nor cruelly demand what the deep rains
And all-involving winds have swept away!

Here the rude clamour of the sportsman's joy,
The gun fast-thundering and the winded horn,
Would tempt the Muse to sing the rural game,
How, in his mid career, the spaniel, struck
Stiff by the tainted gale, with open nose
Outstretched and finely sensible, draws full,
Fearful, and cautious on the latent prey.
As in the sun the circling covey bask
Their varied plumes, and, watchful every way,
Through the rough stubble turn the secret eye.

'Caught in the meshy snare, in vain they beat
Their idle wings, entangled more and more:
Nor, on the surges of the boundless air
Though borne triumphant, are they safe; the gun,
Glanced just, and sudden, from the fowler's eye,
O'ertakes their sounding pinions, and again
Immediate brings them from the towering wing

Dead to the ground; or drives them wide-dispersed,
Wounded and wheeling various down the wind.

These are not subjects for the peaceful muse,
Nor will she stain with such her spotless song—
Then most delighted when she social sees
The whole mixed animal creation round
Alive and happy. 'Tis not joy to her,
This falsely cheerful barbarous game of death,
This rage of pleasure which the restless youth
Awakes, impatient, with the gleaming morn;
When beasts of prey retire that all night long,
Urged by necessity, had ranged the dark,
As if their conscious ravage shunned the light
Ashamed. Not so the steady tyrant, man,
Who, with the thoughtless insolence of power
Inflamed beyond the most infuriate wrath
Of the worst monster that e'er roamed the waste,
For sport alone pursues the cruel chase
Amid the beamings of the gentle days.
Upbraid, ye ravening tribes, our wanton rage,
For hunger kindles you, and lawless want;
But lavish fed, in Nature's bounty rolled,
To joy at anguish, and delight in blood,
Is what your horrid bosoms never knew.

Poor is the triumph o'er the timid hare!
Scared from the corn, and now to some lone seat
Retired-the rushy fen, the ragged furze
Stretched o'er the stony heath, the stubble chapped,
The thistly lawn, the thick entangled broom,
Of the same friendly hue the withered fern,
The fallow ground laid open to the sun
Concoctive, and the nodding sandy bank
Hung o'er the mazes of the mountain brook.
Vain is her best precaution; though she sits
Concealed with folded ears, unsleeping eyes
By Nature raised to take the horizon in,
And head couched close betwixt her hairy feet
In act to spring away. The scented dew
Betrays her early labyrinth; and deep,
In scattered sullen openings, far behind,
With every breeze she hears the coming storm
But, nearer and more frequent as it loads
The sighing gale, she springs amazed, and all
The savage soul of game is up at once—
The pack full-opening various, the shrill horn

Resounded from the hills, the neighing steed
Wild for the chase, and the loud hunter's shout—
O'er a weak, harmless, flying creature, all
Mixed in mad tumult and discordant joy.

The stag, too, singled from the herd, where long
He ranged the branching monarch of the shades,
Before the tempest drives. At first, in speed
He sprightly puts his faith, and, roused by fear,
Gives all his swift aerial soul to flight.
Against the breeze he darts, that way the more
To leave the lessening murderous cry behind.
Deception short! though, fleeter than the winds
Blown o'er the keen-aired mountain by the North,
He bursts the thickets, glances through the glades,
And plunges deep into the wildest wood.
If slow, yet sure, adhesive to the track
Hot-steaming, up behind him come again
The inhuman rout, and from the shady depth
Expel him, circling through his every shift.
He sweeps the forest oft; and sobbing sees
The glades, mild opening to the golden day,
Where in kind contest with his butting friends
He wont to struggle, or his loves enjoy.
Oft in the full-descending flood he tries
To lose the scent, and lave his burning sides—
Oft seeks the herd; the watchful herd, alarmed,
With selfish care avoid a brother's woe.
What shall he do? His once so vivid nerves,
So full of buoyant spirit, now no more
Inspire the course; but fainting, breathless toil
Sick seizes on his heart: he stands at bay,
And puts his last weak refuge in despair.
The big round tears run down his dappled face;
He groans in anguish; while the growling pack,
Blood-happy, hang at his fair jutting chest,
And mark his beauteous chequered sides with gore.

Of this enough. But, if the sylvan youth,
Whose fervent blood boils into violence,
Must have the chase, behold, despising flight,
The roused up lion, resolute and slow,
Advancing full on the protended spear
And coward band that circling wheel aloof.
Slunk from the cavern and the troubled wood,
See the grim wolf; on him his shaggy foe
Vindictive fix, and let the ruffian die:
Or, growling horrid, as the brindled boar

Grins fell destruction, to the monster's heart
Let the dart lighten from the nervous arm.

These Britain knows not; give, ye Britons, then
Your sportive fury pitiless to pour
Loose on the nightly robber of the fold.
Him, from his craggy winding haunts unearthed,
Let all the thunder of the chase pursue.
Throw the broad ditch behind you; o'er the hedge
High bound resistless; nor the deep morass
Refuse, but through the shaking wilderness
Pick your nice way; into the perilous flood
Bear fearless, of the raging instinct full;
And, as you ride the torrent, to the banks
Your triumph sound sonorous, running round
From rock to rock, in circling echo tost;
Then scale the mountains to their woody tops;
Rush down the dangerous steep; and o'er the lawn,
In fancy swallowing up the space between,
Pour all your speed into the rapid game.
For happy he who tops the wheeling chase;
Has every maze evolved, and every guile
Disclosed; who knows the merits of the pack;
Who saw the villain seized, and dying hard
Without complaint, though by an hundred mouths
Relentless torn: O glorious he beyond
His daring peers, when the retreating horn
Calls them to ghostly halls of grey renown,
With woodland honours graced-the fox's fur
Depending decent from the roof, and spread
Round the drear walls, with antic figures fierce,
The stag's large front: he then is loudest heard
When the night staggers with severer toils, With feats
 Thessalian Centaurs never knew,
And their repeated wonders shake the dome

But first the fuelled chimney blazes wide;
The tankards foam; and the strong table groans
Beneath the smoking sirloin, stretched immense
From side to side, in which with desperate knife
They deep incision make, and talk the while
Of England's glory, ne'er to be defaced
While hence they borrow vigour; or, amain
Into the pasty plunged, at intervals,
If stomach keen can intervals allow,
Relating all the glories of the chase.
Then sated Hunger bids his brother Thirst
Produce the mighty bowl: the mighty bowl,

Swelled high with fiery juice, steams liberal round
A potent gale, delicious as the breath
Of Maia to the love-sick shepherdess
On violets diffused, while soft she hears
Her panting shepherd stealing to her arms.
Nor wanting is the brown October, drawn
Mature and perfect from his dark retreat
Of thirty years; and now his honest front
Flames in the light refulgent, not afraid
Even with the vineyard's best produce to vie.
To cheat the thirsty moments, whist a while
Walks his grave round beneath a cloud of smoke,
Wreathed fragrant from the pipe; or the quick dice,
In thunder leaping from the box, awake
The sounding gammon; while romp-loving miss
Is hauled about in gallantry robust.

At last these puling idlenesses laid
Aside, frequent and full, the dry divan
Close in firm circle; and set ardent in
For serious drinking. Nor evasion sly
Nor sober shift is to the puking wretch
Indulged apart; but earnest brimming bowls
Lave every soul, the table floating round,
And pavement faithless to the fuddled foot.
Thus as they swim in mutual swill, the talk,
Vociferous at once from twenty tongues,
Reels fast from theme to theme-from horses, hounds,
To church or mistress, politics or ghost—
In endless mazes, intricate, perplext.
Meantime, with sudden interruption, loud
The impatient catch bursts from the joyous heart.
 That moment touched is each congenial soul;
And, opening in a full-mouthed cry of joy,
The laugh, the slap, the jocund curse goes round;
While, from their slumbers shook, the kennelled hounds
Mix in the music of the day again.
As when the tempest, that has vexed the deep
The dark night long, with fainter murmurs falls;
So gradual sinks their mirth. Their feeble tongues,
Unable to take up the cumbrous word,
Lie quite dissolved. Before their maudlin eyes,
Seen dim and blue, the double tapers dance,
Like the sun wading through the misty sky.
Then, sliding soft, they drop. Confused above,
Glasses and bottles, pipes and gazetteers,
As if the table even itself was drunk,
And steeps them drenched in potent sleep till morn.

Perhaps some doctor of tremendous paunch,
Awful and deep, a black abyss of drink,
Outlives them all; and, from his buried flock
Retiring, full of rumination sad,
Laments the weakness of these latter times.
But if the rougher sex by this fierce sport
Is hurried wild, let not such horrid joy
E'er stain the bosom of the British fair.
Far be the spirit of the chase from them!
Uncomely courage, unbeseeming skill,
To spring the fence, to reign the prancing steed,
The cap, the whip, the masculine attire
In which they roughen to the sense and all
The winning softness of their sex is lost.
In them 'tis graceful to dissolve at woe;
With every motion, every word, to wave
Quick o'er the kindling cheek the ready blush;
And from the smallest violence to shrink
Unequal, then the loveliest in their fears;
And, by this silent adulation soft,
To their protection more engaging man.
O may their eyes no miserable sight,
Save weeping lovers, see! a nobler game,
Through love's enchanting wiles pursued, yet fled,
In chase ambiguous. May their tender limbs
Float in the loose simplicity of dress!
And, fashioned all to harmony, alone
Know they to seize the captivated soul,
In rapture warbled from love-breathing lips;
To teach the lute to languish; with smooth step,
Disclosing motion in its every charm,
To swim along and swell the mazy dance;
To train the foliage o'er the snowy lawn;
To guide the pencil, turn the tuneful page;
To lend new flavour to the fruitful year,
And heighten nature's dainties; in their race
To rear their graces into second life;
To give society its highest taste;
Well-ordered home man's best delight to make;
And, by submissive wisdom, modest skill,
With every gentle care-eluding art,
To raise the virtues, animate the bliss,
Even charm the pains to something more than joy,
And sweeten all the toils of human life:
This be the female dignity and praise.

Ye swains, now hasten to the hazel-bank,
Where down yon dale the wildly-winding brook

Falls hoarse from steep to steep. In close array,
Fit for the thickets and the tangling shrub,
Ye virgins, come. For you their latest song
The woodlands raise; the clustering nuts for you
The lover finds amid the secret shade;
And, where they burnish on the topmost bough,
With active vigour crushes down the tree;
Or shakes them ripe from the resigning husk,
A glossy shower and of an ardent brown
As are the ringlets of Melinda's hair—
Melinda! form'd with every grace complete,
Yet these neglecting, above beauty wise,
And far transcending such a vulgar praise.

Hence from the busy joy-resounding fields,
In cheerful error let us tread the maze
Of Autumn unconfined; and taste, revived,
The breath of orchard big with bending fruit.
Obedient to the breeze and beating ray,
From the deep-loaded bough a mellow shower
Incessant melts away. The juicy pear
Lies in a soft profusion scattered round.
A various sweetness swells the gentle race,
By Nature's all-refining hand prepared,
Of tempered sun, and water, earth, and air,
In ever-changing composition mixed.
Such, falling frequent through the chiller night,
The fragrant stores, the wide-projected heaps
Of apples, which the lusty-handed year
Innumerous o'er the blushing orchard shakes.
A various spirit, fresh, delicious, keen,
Dwells in their gelid pores, and active points
The piercing cider for the thirsty tongue—
Thy native theme, and boon inspirer too,
Phillips, Pomona's bard! the second thou
Who nobly durst in rhyme-unfettered verse
With British freedom sing the British song—
How from Silurian vats high-sparkling wines
Foam in transparent floods, some strong to cheer
The wintry revels of the labouring hind,
And tasteful some to cool the summer hours.

In this glad season, while his sweetest beams
The Sun sheds equal o'er the meekened day,
Oh, lose me in the green delightful walks
Of, Dodington, thy seat, serene and plain;
Where simple Nature reigns; and every view

Diffusive spreads the pure Dorsetian downs
In boundless prospect-yonder shagged with wood,
Here rich with harvest, and there white with flocks!
Meantime the grandeur of thy lofty dome
Far-splendid seizes on the ravished eye.
New beauties rise with each revolving day;
New columns swell; and still the fresh Spring finds
New plants to quicken, and new groves to green.
Full of thy genius all, the Muses' seat!
Where, in the secret bower and winding walk,
For virtuous Young and thee they twine the bay.
Here wandering oft, fired with the restless thirst
Of thy applause, I solitary court
The inspiring breeze, and meditate the book
Of Nature, ever open, aiming thence
Warm from the heart to learn the moral song.
And, as I steal along the sunny wall,
Where Autumn basks, with fruit empurpled deep,
My pleasing theme continual prompts my thoughts—
Presents the downy peach, the shining plum
With a fine bluish mist of animals
Clouded, the ruddy nectarine, and dark
Beneath his ample leaf the luscious fig.
The vine too here her curling tendrils shoots,
Hangs out her clusters glowing to the south,
And scarcely wishes for a warmer sky.

Turn we a moment fancy's rapid flight
To vigorous soils and climes of fair extent,
Where, by the potent sun elated high,
The vineyard swells refulgent on the day,
Spreads o'er the vale, or up the mountain climbs
Profuse, and drinks amid the sunny rocks,
From cliff to cliff increased, the heightened blaze.
Low bend the weighty boughs. The clusters clear,
Half through the foliage seen, or ardent flame
Or shine transparent; while perfection breathes
White o'er the turgent film the living dew.
As thus they brighten with exalted juice,
Touched into flavour by the mingling ray,
The rural youth and virgins o'er the field,
Each fond for each to cull the autumnal prime,
Exulting rove, and speak the vintage nigh.
Then comes the crushing swain; the country floats,
And foams unbounded with the mashy flood,
That, by degrees fermented, and refined,
Round the raised nations pours the cup of joy—
The claret smooth, red as the lip we press

In sparkling fancy while we drain the bowl,
The mellow-tasted burgundy, and, quick
As is the wit it gives, the gay champagne.

Now, by the cool declining year condensed,
Descend the copious exhalations, checked
As up the middle sky unseen they stole,
And roll the doubling fogs around the hill.
No more the mountain, horrid, vast, sublime,
Who pours a sweep of rivers from his sides,
And high between contending kingdoms rears
The rocky long division, fills the view
With great variety; but, in a night
Of gathering vapour, from the baffled sense
Sinks dark and dreary. Thence expanding far,
The huge dusk gradual swallows up the plain:
Vanish the woods: the dim-seen river seems,
Sullen and slow, to roll the misty wave.
Even in the height of noon oppressed, the sun
Sheds, weak and blunt, his wide-refracted ray;
Whence glaring oft, with many a broadened orb,
He frights the nations .Indistinct on earth,
Seen through the turbid air, beyond the life
Objects appear, and, wildered, o'er the waste
The shepherd stalks gigantic; till at last,
Wreathed dun around, in deeper circles still
Successive closing, sits the general fog
Unbounded o'er the world, and, mingling thick,
A formless grey confusion covers all.
As when of old (so sung the Hebrew bard)
Light, uncollected, through the Chaos urged
Its infant way, nor order yet had drawn
His lovely train from out the dubious gloom.

These roving mists, that constant now begin
To smoke along the hilly country, these,
With weighty rains and melted Alpine snows.
The mountain-cisterns fill-those ample stores
Of water, scooped among the hollow rocks,
Whence gush the streams, the ceaseless fountains play,
And their unfailing wealth the rivers draw.
Some sages say, that, where the numerous wave
For ever lashes the resounding shore,
Drilled through the sandy stratum, every way,
The waters with the sandy stratum rise;
Amid whose angles infinitely strained,
They joyful leave their jaggy salts behind,
And clear-and sweeten as they soak along.

Nor stops the restless fluid, mounting still,
Though oft amidst the irriguous vale it springs;
But, to the mountain courted by the sand,
That leads it darkling on in faithful maze,
Far from the parent main, it boils again
Fresh into day, and all the glittering hill
Is bright with spouting rills. But hence this vain
Amusive dream! why should the waters love
To take so far a journey to the hills,
When the sweet valleys offer to their toil
Inviting quiet and a nearer bed?
Or if, by blind ambition led astray,
They must aspire, why should they sudden stop
Among the broken mountain's rushy dells.
And, ere they gain its highest peak, desert
The attractive sand that charmed their course so long?
Besides, the hard agglomerating salts,
The spoil of ages, would impervious choke
Their secret channels, or by slow degrees,
High as the hills, protrude the swelling vales:
Old ocean too, sucked through the porous globe,
Had long ere now forsook his horrid bed,
And brought Deucalion's watery times again.

Say, then, where lurk the vast eternal springs
That, like creating Nature, lie concealed
From mortal eye, yet with their lavish stores
Refresh the globe and all its joyous tribes?

O thou pervading genius, given to man
To trace the secrets of the dark abyss!
Oh! lay the mountains bare, and wide display
Their hidden structure to the astonished view;
Strip from the branching Alps their piny load,
The huge incumbrance of horrific woods
From Asian Taurus, from Imaus stretched
Athwart the roving Tartar's sullen bounds;
Give opening Hemus to my searching eye,
And high Olympus pouring many a stream!
Oh, from the sounding summits of the north,
The Dofrine Hills, through Scandinavia rolled
To farthest Lapland and the frozen main;
From lofty Caucasus, far seen by those
Who in the Caspian and black Euxine toil;
From cold Riphaean rocks, which the wild Russ
Believes the stony girdle of the world;
And all the dreadful mountains wrapt in storm
Whence wide Siberia draws her lonely floods;

Oh, sweep the eternal snows! Hung o'er the deep,
 That ever works beneath his sounding base,
Bid Atlas, propping heaven, as poets feign,
His subterranean wonders spread! Unveil
 The miny caverns, blazing on the day,
Of Abyssinia's cloud-compelling cliffs,
And of the bending Mountains of the Moon!
O'ertopping all these giant-sons of earth,
Let the dire Andes, from the radiant Line
Stretched to the stormy seas that thunder round
The Southern Pole, their hideous deeps unfold!
Amazing scene! Behold! the glooms disclose!
I see the rivers in their infant beds!
Deep, deep I hear them labouring to get free!
I see the leaning strata, artful ranged;
The gaping fissures, to receive the rains,
The melting snows, and ever-dripping fogs.

Strowed bibulous above I see the sands,
The pebbly gravel next, the layers then
Of mingled moulds, of more retentive earths,
The guttured rocks and mazy-running clefts,
That, while the stealing moisture they transmit,
Retard its motion, and forbid its waste.
Beneath the incessant weeping of these drains,
I see the rocky siphons stretched immense,
The mighty reservoirs, of hardened chalk
Or stiff compacted clay capacious formed:
O'erflowing thence, the congregated stores,
The crystal treasures of the liquid world,
Through the stirred sands a bubbling passage burst,
And, welling out around the middle steep
Or from the bottoms of the bosomed hills
In pure effusion flow. United thus,
The exhaling sun, the vapour-burdened air,
The gelid mountains, that to rain condensed
These vapours in continual current draw,
And send them o'er the fair-divided earth
In bounteous rivers to the deep again,
A social commerce hold, and firm support
The full-adjusted harmony of things.

When Autumn scatters his departing gleams,
Warned of approaching Winter, gathered, play
The swallow-people; and, tossed wide around,
O'er the calm sky in convolution swift
The feathered eddy floats, rejoicing once
Ere to their wintry slumbers they retire,

In clusters clung beneath the mouldering bank,
And where, unpierced by frost, the cavern sweats:
Or rather, into warmer climes conveyed,
And now, their route designed, their leaders chose,
Their tribes adjusted, cleaned their vigorous wings,
And many a circle, many a short essay,
Wheeled round and round, in congregation full
The figured flight ascends, and, riding high
The aerial billows, mixes with the clouds.

Or, where the Northern Ocean in vast whirls
Boils round the naked melancholy isles
Of farthest Thule, and the Atlantic surge
Pours in among the stormy Hebrides,
Who can recount what transmigrations there
Are annual made? what nations come and go?
And how the living clouds on clouds arise,
Infinite wings! till all the plume-dark air
And rude resounding shore are one wild cry?

Here the plain harmless native his small flock
And herd diminutive of many hues
Tends on the little island's verdant swell,
The shepherd's sea-girt reign; or, to the rocks
Dire-clinging, gathers his ovarious food;
Or sweeps the fishy shore; or treasures up
The plumage, rising full, to form the bed
Of luxury. And here a while the muse,
High hovering o'er the broad cerulean scene,
Sees Caledonia in romantic view—
Her airy mountains from the waving main
Invested with a keen diffusive sky,
Breathing the soul acute; her forests huge,
Incult, robust, and tall, by Nature's hand
Planted of old; her azure lakes between,
Poured out extensive, and of watery wealth
Full; winding deep and green, her fertile vales,
With many a cool translucent brimming flood
Washed lovely, from the Tweed (pure parent-stream,
Whose pastoral banks first heard my Doric reed,
With, silvan Jed, thy tributary brook)
To where the north-inflated tempest foams
O'er Orca's or Betubium's highest peak—
Nurse of a people, in misfortune's school
Trained up to hardy deeds, soon visited
By Learning, when before the Gothic rage
She took her western flight; a manly race
Of unsubmitting spirit, wise, and brave,

Who still through bleeding ages struggled hard
(As well unhappy Wallace can attest,
Great patriot-hero! ill requited chief!)
To hold a generous undiminished state,
Too much in vain! Hence, of unequal bounds
Impatient, and by tempting glory borne
O'er every land, for every land their life
Has flowed profuse, their piercing genius planned,
And swelled the pomp of peace their faithful toil:
As from their own clear north in radiant streams
Bright over Europe bursts the boreal morn.

Oh! is there not some patriot in whose power
That best, that godlike luxury is placed,
Of blessing thousands, thousands yet unborn,
Through late posterity? some, large of soul,
To cheer dejected Industry, to give
A double harvest to the pining swain,
And teach the labouring hand the sweets of toil?
How, by the finest art, the native robe
To weave; how, white as Hyperborean snow,
To form the lucid lawn; with venturous oar
How to dash wide the billow; nor look on,
Shamefully passive, while Batavian fleets
Defraud us of the glittering finny swarms
That heave our friths and crowd upon our shores;
How all-enlivening trade to rouse, and wing
The prosperous sail from every growing port,
Uninjured, round the sea-encircled globe;
And thus, in soul united as in name,
Bid Britain reign the mistress of the deep?

Yes, there are such. And full on thee, Argyle,
Her hope, her stay, her darling, and her boast,
From her first patriots and her heroes sprung,
Thy fond imploring Country turns her eye;
In thee, with all a mother's triumph, sees
Her every virtue, every grace combined,
Her genius, wisdom, her engaging turn,
Her pride of honour, and her courage tried,
Calm and intrepid, in the very throat
Of sulphurous war, on Tenier's dreadful field.
Nor less the palm of peace enwreathes thy brow:
For, powerful as thy sword, from thy rich tongue
Persuasion flows, and wins the high debate;
While mixed in thee combine the charm of youth,
The force of manhood, and the depth of age.
Thee, Forbes, too, whom every worth attends,

As truth sincere, as weeping friendship kind,
Thee, truly generous, and in silence great,
Thy country feels through her reviving arts,
Planned by thy wisdom, by thy soul informed;
And seldom has she felt a friend like thee.

But see the fading many-coloured woods,
Shade deepening over shade, the country round
Imbrown; a crowded umbrage, dusk and dun,
Of every hue from wan declining green
To sooty dark. These now the lonesome muse,
Low-whispering, lead into their leaf-strown walks,
And give the season in its latest view.

Meantime, light shadowing all, a sober calm
Fleeces unbounded ether; whose least wave
Stands tremulous, uncertain where to turn
The gentle current; while, illumined wide,
The dewy-skirted clouds imbibe the sun,
And through their lucid veil his softened force
Shed o'er the peaceful world. Then is the time
For those whom wisdom and whom nature charm
To steal themselves from the degenerate crowd,
And soar above this little scene of things—
To tread low-thoughted vice beneath their feet,
To soothe the throbbing passions into peace,
And woo lone Quiet in her silent walks.

Thus solitary, and in pensive guise,
Oft let me wander o'er the russet mead,
And through the saddened grove, where scarce is heard
One dying strain to cheer the woodman's toil.
Haply some widowed songster pours his plaint
Far in faint warblings through the tawny copse;
While congregated thrushes, linnets, larks,
And each wild throat whose artless strains so late
Swelled all the music of the swarming shades,
Robbed of their tuneful souls, now shivering sit
On the dead tree, a dull despondent flock,
With not a brightness waving o'er their plumes,
And naught save chattering discord in their note.
Oh, let not, aimed from some inhuman eye,
The gun the music of the coming year
Destroy, and harmless, unsuspecting harm,
Lay the weak tribes, a miserable prey!
In mingled murder fluttering on the ground!

The pale descending year, yet pleasing still,

A gentler mood inspires; for now the leaf
Incessant rustles from the mournful grove,
Oft startling such as studious walk below,
And slowly circles through the waving air.
But, should a quicker breeze amid the boughs
Sob, o'er the sky the leafy deluge streams;
Till, choked and matted with the dreary shower,
The forest-walks, at every rising gale,
Roll wide the wither'd waste, and whistle bleak.
Fled is the blasted verdure of the fields;
And, shrunk into their beds, the flowery race
Their sunny robes resign. Even what remained
Of bolder fruits falls from the naked tree;
And-woods, fields, gardens, orchards, all around—
The desolated prospect thrills the soul.

He comes! he comes! in every breeze the Power
Of Philosophic Melancholy comes!
His near approach the sudden-starting tear,
The glowing cheek, the mild dejected air,
The softened feature, and the beating heart,
Pierced deep with many a virtuous pang, declare.
O'er all the soul his sacred influence breathes;
Inflames imagination; through the breast
Infuses every tenderness; and far
Beyond dim earth exalts the swelling thought.
Ten thousand thousand fleet ideas, such
As never mingled with the vulgar dream,
Crowd fast into the mind's creative eye.
As fast the correspondent passions rise,
As varied, and as high-devotion raised
To rapture, and divine astonishment;
The love of nature unconfined, and, chief,
Of human race; the large ambitious wish
To make them blest; the sigh for suffering worth
Lost in obscurity; the noble scorn
Of tyrant pride; the fearless great resolve;
The wonder which the dying patriot draws,
Inspiring glory through remotest time;
The awakened throb for virtue and for fame;
The sympathies of love and friendship dear,
With all the social offspring of the heart.

Oh! bear me then to vast embowering shades,
To twilight groves, and visionary vales,
To weeping grottoes, and prophetic glooms;
Where angel forms athwart the solemn dusk,
Tremendous, sweep, or seem to sweep along;

And voices more than human, through the void
Deep-sounding, seize the enthusiastic ear.

Or is this gloom too much? Then lead, ye Powers
That o'er the garden and the rural seat
Preside, which, shining through the cheerful land
In countless numbers, blest Britannia sees—
Oh! lead me to the wide extended walks,
The fair majestic paradise of Stowe!
Not Persian Cyrus on Ionia's shore
E'er saw such sylvan scenes, such various art
By genius fired, such ardent genius tamed
By cool judicious art, that in the strife
All-beauteous Nature fears to be outdone.
And there, O Pitt! thy country's early boast,
There let me sit beneath the sheltered slopes,
Or in that Temple where, in future times,
Thou well shalt merit a distinguished name,
And, with thy converse blest, catch the last smiles
Of Autumn beaming o'er the yellow woods.
While there with thee the enchanted round I walk,
The regulated wild, gay fancy then
Will tread in thought the groves of Attic land;
Will from thy standard taste refine her own,
Correct her pencil to the purest truth
Of nature, or, the unimpassioned shades
Forsaking, raise it to the human mind.
Oh, if hereafter she with juster hand
Shall draw the tragic scene, instruct her thou
To mark the varied movements of the heart,
What every decent character requires,
And every passion speaks! Oh, through her strain
Breathe thy pathetic eloquence, that moulds
The attentive senate, charms, persuades, exalts,
Of honest zeal the indignant lightning throws,
And shakes Corruption on her venal throne!

While thus we talk, and through Elysian vales
Delighted rove, perhaps a sigh escapes—
What pity, Cobham! thou thy verdant files
Of ordered trees shouldst here inglorious range,
Instead of squadrons flaming o'er the field,
And long-embattled hosts! when the proud foe,
The faithless vain disturber of mankind,
Insulting Gaul, has roused the world to war;
When keen, once more, within their bounds to press
Those polished robbers, those ambitious slaves,
The British youth would hail thy wise command,

Thy tempered ardour and thy veteran skill.

The western sun withdraws the shortened day;
And humid evening, gliding o'er the sky,
In her chill progress, to the ground condensed
The vapours throws. Where creeping waters ooze,
Where marshes stagnate, and where rivers wind,
Cluster the rolling fogs, and swim along
The dusky-mantled lawn. Meanwhile the moon,
Full-orbed and breaking through the scattered clouds,
Shows her broad visage in the crimsoned east.
Turned to the sun direct, her spotted disk
(Where mountains rise, umbrageous dales descend,
And caverns deep, as optic tube descries)
A smaller earth, gives all his blaze again,
Void of its flame, and sheds a softer day.
Now through the passing cloud she seems to stoop,
Now up the pure cerulean rides sublime.
Wide the pale deluge floats, and streaming mild
O'er the skied mountain to the shadowy vale,
While rocks and floods reflect the quivering gleam,
The whole air whitens with a boundless tide
Of silver radiance trembling round the world.

But when, half blotted from the sky, her light
Fainting, permits the starry fires to burn
With keener lustre through the depth of heaven;
Or quite extinct her deadened orb appears,
And scarce appears, of sickly beamless white;
Oft in this season, silent from the north
A blaze of meteors shoots-ensweeping first
The lower skies, they all at once converge
High to the crown of heaven, and, all at once
Relapsing quick, as quickly re-ascend,
And mix and thwart, extinguish and renew,
All ether coursing in a maze of light.

From look to look, contagious through the crowd,
The panic runs, and into wondrous shapes
The appearance throws-armies in meet array,
Thronged with aerial spears and steeds of fire;
Till, the long lines of full-extended war
In bleeding fight commixed, the sanguine flood
Rolls a broad slaughter o'er the plains of heaven.
As thus they scan the visionary scene,
On all sides swells the superstitious din,
Incontinent; and busy frenzy talks
Of blood and battle; cities overturned,

And late at night in swallowing earthquake sunk,
Or hideous wrapt in fierce ascending flame;
Of sallow famine, inundation, storm;
Of pestilence, and every great distress;
Empires subversed, when ruling fate has struck
The unalterable hour: even nature's self
Is deemed to totter on the brink of time.
Not so the man of philosophic eye
And inspect sage: the waving brightness he
Curious surveys, inquisitive to know
The causes and materials, yet unfixed,
Of this appearance beautiful and new.

Now black and deep the night begins to fall,
A shade immense! Sunk in the quenching gloom,
Magnificent and vast, are heaven and earth.
Order confounded lies, all beauty void,
Distinction lost, and gay variety
One universal blot-such the fair power
Of light, to kindle and create the whole.
Drear is the state of the benighted wretch
Who then bewildered wanders through the dark
Full of pale fancies and chimeras huge;
Nor visited by one directive ray
From cottage streaming or from airy hall.
Perhaps, impatient as he stumbles on,
Struck from the root of slimy rushes, blue
The wild-fire scatters round, or, gathered, trails
A length of flame deceitful o'er the moss;
Whither decoyed by the fantastic blaze,
Now lost and now renewed, he sinks absorbed,
Rider and horse, amid the miry gulf—
While still, from day to day, his pining wife
And plaintive children his return await,
In wild conjecture lost. At other times,
Sent by the better genius of the night,
Innoxious, gleaming on the horse's mane,
The meteor sits, and shows the narrow path
That winding leads through pits of death, or else
Instructs him how to take the dangerous ford.

The lengthened night elapsed, the morning shines
Serene, in all her dewy beauty bright,
Unfolding fair the last autumnal day.
And now the mounting sun dispels the fog;
The rigid hoar-frost melts before his beam;
And, hung on every spray, on every blade
Of grass, the myriad dew-drops twinkle round.

Ah, see where, robbed and murdered, in that pit
Lies the still-heaving hive! at evening snatched,
Beneath the cloud of guilt-concealing night,
And fixed o'er sulphur-while, not dreaming ill,
The happy people in their waxen cells
Sat tending public cares and planning schemes
Of temperance for Winter poor; rejoiced
To mark, full-flowing round, their copious stores.
Sudden the dark oppressive steam ascends;
And, used to milder scents, the tender race
By thousands tumbles from their honeyed domes,
Convolved and agonizing in the dust.
And was it then for this you roamed the spring,
Intent from flower to flower? for this you toiled
Ceaseless the burning summer-heats away?
For this in Autumn searched the blooming waste,
Nor lost one sunny gleam? for this sad fate?
O man! tyrannic lord! how long, how long
Shall prostrate nature groan beneath your rage,
Awaiting renovation? When obliged,
Must you destroy? Of their ambrosial food
Can you not borrow, and in just return
Afford them shelter from the wintry winds?
Or, as the sharp year pinches, with their own
Again regale them on some smiling day?
See where the stony bottom of their town
Looks desolate and wild,-with here and there
A helpless number, who the ruined state
Survive, lamenting weak, cast out to death!
Thus a proud city, populous and rich.
Full of the works of peace, and high in joy,
At theatre or feast, or sunk in sleep
(As late, Palermo, was thy fate) is seized
By some dread earthquake, and convulsive hurled
Sheer from the black foundation, stench-involved,
Into a gulf of blue sulphureous flame.

Hence every harsher sight! for now the day,
O'er heaven and earth diffused, grows warm and high;
Infinite splendour! wide-investing all.
How still the breeze! save what the filmy threads
Of dew evaporate brushes from the plain.
How clear the cloudless sky! how deeply tinged
With a peculiar blue! the ethereal arch
How swelled immense! amid whose azure throned,
The radiant sun how gay! how calm below
The gilded earth! the harvest-treasures all

Now, gathered in, beyond the rage of storms,
Sure to the swain; the circling fence shut up;
And instant Winter's utmost rage defied—
While, loose to festive joy, the country round
Laughs with the loud sincerity of mirth,
Shook to the wind their cares. The toil-strung youth,
By the quick sense of music taught alone,
Leaps wildly graceful in the lively dance.
Her every charm abroad, the village-toast,
Young, buxom, warm, in native beauty rich,
Darts not-unmeaning looks; and, where her eye
Points an approving smile, with double force
The cudgel rattles, and the wrestler twines.
Age too shines out; and, garrulous, recounts
The feats of youth. Thus they rejoice; nor think
That with to-morrow's sun their annual toil
Begins again the never-ceasing round.

Oh! knew he but his happiness, of men
The happiest he! who far from public rage
Deep in the vale, with a choice few retired;
Drinks the pure pleasures of the rural life.
What though the dome be wanting, whose proud gate
Each morning vomits out the sneaking crowd
Of flatterers false, and in their turn abused?
Vile intercourse! What though the glittering robe,
Of every hue reflected light can give,
Or floating loose or stiff with massy gold,
The pride and gaze of fools, oppress him not?
What though, from utmost land and sea purveyed,
For him each rarer tributary life
Bleeds not, and his insatiate table heaps
With luxury and death? What though his bowl
Flames not with costly juice; nor, sunk in beds
Oft of gay care, he tosses out the night,
Or melts the thoughtless hours in idle state?
What though he knows not those fantastic joys
That still amuse the wanton, still deceive;
A face of pleasure, but a heart of pain;
Their hollow moments undelighted all?
Sure peace is his; a solid life, estranged
To disappointment and fallacious hope—
Rich in content, in Nature's bounty rich,
In herbs and fruits; whatever greens the spring
When heaven descends in showers, or bends the bough
When summer reddens and when autumn beams,
Or in the wintry glebe whatever lies
Concealed and fattens with the richest sap:

These are not wanting; nor the milky drove,
Luxuriant spread o'er all the lowing vale;
Nor bleating mountains; nor the chide of streams
And hum of bees, inviting sleep sincere
Into the guiltless breast beneath the shade,
Or thrown at large amid the fragrant hay;
Nor aught besides of prospect, grove, or song,
Dim grottoes, gleaming lakes, and fountain clear.
Here too dwells simple truth, plain innocence,
Unsullied beauty, sound unbroken youth
Patient of labour-with a little pleased,
Health ever-blooming, unambitious toil,
Calm contemplation, and poetic ease.

Let others brave the flood in quest of gain,
And beat for joyless months the gloomy wave.
Let such as deem it glory to destroy
Rush into blood, the sack of cities seek—
Unpierced, exulting in the widow's wail,
The virgin's shriek, and infant's trembling cry.
Let some, far distant from their native soil,
Urged or by want or hardened avarice,
Find other lands beneath another sun.
Let this through cities work his eager way
By legal outrage and established guile,
The social sense extinct; and that ferment
Mad into tumult the seditious herd,
Or melt them down to slavery. Let these
Ensnare the wretched in the toils of law,
Fomenting discord, and perplexing right,
An iron race! and those of fairer front,
But equal inhumanity, in courts,
Delusive pomp, and dark cabals delight;
Wreathe the deep bow, diffuse the lying smile,
And tread the weary labyrinth of state.
While he, from all the stormy passions free
That restless men involve, hears, and but hears,
At distance safe, the human tempest roar,
Wrapped close in conscious peace. The fall of kings,
The rage of nations, and the crush of states
Move not the man who, from the world escaped,
In still retreats and flowery solitudes
To Nature's voice attends from month to month,
And day to day, through the revolving year
Admiring, sees her in her every shape;
Feels all her sweet emotions at his heart;
Takes what she liberal gives, nor thinks of more.
He, when young Spring protrudes the bursting gems,

Marks the first bud, and sucks the healthful gale
Into his freshened soul; her genial hours
He full enjoys; and not a beauty blows

And not an opening blossom breathes in vain.
In Summer he, beneath the living shade,
Such as o'er frigid Tempe wont to wave,
Or Haemus cool, reads what the muse, of these
Perhaps, has in immortal numbers sung;
Or what she dictates writes; and oft, an eye
Shot round, rejoices in the vigorous year.
When Autumn's yellow lustre gilds the world
And tempts the sickled swain into the field,
Seized by the general joy his heart distends,
With gentle throes; and, through the tepid gleams
Deep musing, then he best exerts his song.
Even Winter wild to him is full of bliss.
The mighty tempest, and the hoary waste
Abrupt and deep, stretched o'er the buried earth,
Awake to solemn thought. At night the skies,
Disclosed and kindled by refining frost,
Pour every lustre on the exalted eye.
A friend, a book the stealing hours secure,
And mark them down for wisdom. With swift wing,
O'er land and sea imagination roams;
Or truth, divinely breaking on his mind,
Elates his being, and unfolds his powers;
Or in his breast heroic virtue burns.
The touch of kindred, too, and love he feels—
The modest eye whose beams on his alone
Ecstatic shine, the little strong embrace
Of prattling children, twined around his neck,
And emulous to please him, calling forth
The fond parental soul. Nor purpose gay,
Amusement, dance, or song, he sternly scorns:
For happiness and true philosophy
Are of the social still and smiling kind.
This is the life which those who fret in guilt
And guilty cities never knew-the life
Led by primeval ages uncorrupt
When angels dwelt, and God himself, with man!

O Nature! all-sufficient! over all
Enrich me with the knowledge of thy works;
Snatch me to heaven; thy rolling wonders there,
World beyond world, in infinite extent
Profusely scattered o'er the blue immense,
Show me; their motions, periods, and their laws

Give me to scan; through the disclosing deep
Light my blind way: the mineral strata there;
Thrust blooming thence the vegetable world;
O'er that the rising system, more complex,
Of animals; and, higher still, the mind,
The varied scene of quick-compounded thought,
And where the mixing passions endless shift;
These ever open to my ravished eye—
A search, the flight of time can ne'er exhaust!
But, if to that unequal-if the blood
In sluggish streams about my heart forbid
That best ambition-under closing shades
Inglorious lay me by the lowly brook,
And whisper to my dreams. From thee begin,
Dwell all on thee, with thee conclude my song;
And let me never, never stray from thee!

WINTER

THE ARGUMENT

The subject proposed. Address to the Earl of Wilmington. First approach of Winter. According to the natural course of the season, various storms described. Rain. Wind, Snow. The driving of the snows: a man perishing among them; whence reflections on the wants and miseries of human life. The wolves descending from the Alps and Apennines. A winter evening described: as spent by philosophers; by the country people; in the city. Frost. A view of Winter within the polar circle. A thaw. The whole concluding with moral reflections on a future state.

See, Winter comes to rule the varied year,
Sullen and sad, with all his rising train—
Vapours, and clouds, and storms. Be these my theme;
These, that exalt the soul to solemn thought
And heavenly musing. Welcome, kindred glooms!
Cogenial horrors, hail! With frequent foot,
Pleased have I, in my cheerful morn of life,
When nursed by careless solitude I lived
And sung of Nature with unceasing joy,
Pleased have I wandered through your rough domain;
Trod the pure virgin-snows, myself as pure;
Heard the winds roar, and the big torrent burst;
Or seen the deep-fermenting tempest brewed
In the grim evening-sky. Thus passed the time,
Till through the lucid chambers of the south
Looked out the joyous Spring-looked out and smiled

To thee, the patron of this first essay,
The Muse, O Wilmington! renews her song.
Since has she rounded the revolving year:
Skimm'd the gay Spring; on eagle-pinions borne,
Attempted through the Summer-blaze to rise;
Then swept o'er Autumn with the shadowy gale.
And now among the Wintry clouds again,
Rolled in the doubling storm, she tries to soar,
To swell her note with all the rushing winds,
To suit her sounding cadence to the floods;
As is her theme, her numbers wildly great.
Thrice happy, could she fill thy judging ear
With bold description and with manly thought!
Nor art thou skilled in awful schemes alone,
And how to make a mighty people thrive;
But equal goodness, sound integrity,
A firm, unshaken, uncorrupted soul
Amid a sliding age, and burning strong,
Not vainly blazing, for thy country's weal,
A steady spirit, regularly free—
These, each exalting each, the statesman light
Into the patriot; these, the public hope
And eye to thee converting, bid the Muse
Record what envy dares not flattery call.

Now, when the cheerless empire of the sky
To Capricorn the Centaur-Archer yields,
And fierce Aquarius stains the inverted year—
Hung o'er the farthest verge of heaven, the sun
Scarce spreads o'er ether the dejected day.
Faint are his gleams, and ineffectual shoot
His struggling rays in horizontal lines
Through the thick air; as clothed in cloudy storm,
Weak, wan, and broad, he skirts the southern sky;
And, soon descending, to the long dark night,
Wide-shading all, the prostrate world resigns.
Nor is the night unwished; while vital heat,
Light, life, and joy the dubious day forsake.
Meantime, in sable cincture, shadows vast,
Deep-tinged and damp, and congregated clouds,
And all the vapoury turbulence of heaven
Involve the face of things. Thus Winter falls,
A heavy gloom oppressive o'er the world,
Through Nature shedding influence malign,
And rouses up the seeds of dark disease.
The soul of man dies in him, loathing life,
And black with more than melancholy views.
The cattle droop; and o'er the furrowed land,

Fresh from the plough, the dun discoloured flocks,
Untended spreading, crop the wholesome root.
Along the woods, along the moorish fens,
Sighs the sad genius of the coming storm;
And up among the loose disjointed cliffs
And fractured mountains wild, the brawling brook
And cave, presageful, send a hollow moan,
Resounding long in listening fancy's ear.

Then comes the father of the tempest forth,
Wrapt in black glooms. First, joyless rains obscure
Drive through the mingling skies with vapour foul,
Dash on the mountain's brow, and shake the woods
That grumbling wave below. The unsightly plain
Lies a brown deluge; as the low-bent clouds
Pour flood on flood, yet unexhausted still
Combine, and, deepening into night, shut up
The day's fair face. The wanderers of heaven,
Each to his home, retire; save those that love
To take their pastime in the troubled air,
Or skimming flutter round the dimply pool.
The cattle from the untasted fields return
And ask, with meaning low, their wonted stalls,
Or ruminate in the contiguous shade.
Thither the household feathery people crowd,
The crested cock, with all his female train,
Pensive and dripping; while the cottage-hind
Hangs o'er the enlivening blaze, and taleful there
Recounts his simple frolic: much he talks,
And much he laughs, nor recks the storm that blows
Without, and rattles on his humble roof.

Wide o'er the brim, with many a torrent swelled,
And the mixed ruin of its banks o'erspread,
At last the roused-up river pours along:
Resistless, roaring, dreadful, down it comes,
From the rude mountain and the mossy wild,
Tumbling through rocks abrupt, and sounding far;
Then o'er the sanded valley floating spreads,
Calm, sluggish, silent; till again, constrained
Between two meeting hills, it bursts a way
Where rocks and woods o'erhang the turbid stream;
There, gathering triple force, rapid and deep,
It boils, and wheels, and foams, and thunders through.

Nature! great parent! whose unceasing hand
Rolls round the Seasons of the changeful year,
How mighty, how majestic are thy works!

With what a pleasing dread they swell the soul,
That sees astonished, and astonished sings!
Ye too, ye winds! that now begin to blow
With boisterous sweep, I raise my voice to you.
Where are your stores, ye powerful beings! say,
Where your aerial magazines reserved
To swell the brooding terrors of the storm?
In what far-distant region of the sky,
Hushed in deep silence, sleep you when 'tis calm?

When from the pallid sky the Sun descends,
With many a spot, that o'er his glaring orb
Uncertain wanders, stained; red fiery streaks
Begin to flush around. The reeling clouds
Stagger with dizzy poise, as doubting yet
Which master to obey; while, rising slow,
Blank in the leaden-coloured east, the moon
Wears a wan circle round her blunted horns.
Seen through the turbid, fluctuating air,
The stars obtuse emit a shivering ray;
Or frequent seem to shoot athwart the gloom,
And long behind them trail the whitening blaze.
Snatched in short eddies, plays the withered leaf;
And on the flood the dancing feather floats.
With broadened nostrils to the sky upturned,
The conscious heifer snuffs the stormy gale.
Even, as the matron, at her nightly task,
With pensive labour draws the flaxen thread,
The wasted taper and the crackling flame
Foretell the blast. But chief the plumy race,
The tenants of the sky, its changes speak.
Retiring from the downs, where all day long
They picked their scanty fare, a blackening train
Of clamorous rooks thick-urge their weary flight,
And seek the closing shelter of the grove.
Assiduous, in his bower, the wailing owl
Plies his sad song. The cormorant on high
Wheels from the deep, and screams along the land.
Loud shrieks the soaring hern; and with wild wing
The circling sea-fowl cleave the flaky clouds.
Ocean, unequal pressed, with broken tide
And blind commotion heaves; while from the shore,
Eat into caverns by the restless wave,
And forest-rustling mountain comes a voice
That, solemn-sounding, bids the world prepare.
Then issues forth the storm with sudden burst,
And hurls the whole precipitated air
Down in a torrent. On the passive main

Descends the ethereal force, and with strong gust
Turns from its bottom the discoloured deep.
Through the black night that sits immense around,
Lashed into foam, the fierce-conflicting brine
Seems o'er a thousand raging waves to burn.
Meantime the mountain-billows, to the clouds
In dreadful tumult swelled, surge above surge,
Burst into chaos with tremendous roar,
And anchored navies from their stations drive
Wild as the winds, across the howling waste
Of mighty waters: now the inflated wave
Straining they scale, and now impetuous shoot
Into the secret chambers of the deep,
The wintry Baltic thundering o'er their head.
Emerging thence again, before the breath
Of full-exerted heaven they wing their course,
And dart on distant coasts-if some sharp rock
Or shoal insidious break not their career,
And in loose fragments fling them floating round.

Nor less at land the loosened tempest reigns.
The mountain thunders, and its sturdy sons
Stoop to the bottom of the rocks they shade.
Lone on the midnight steep, and all aghast,
The dark wayfaring stranger breathless toils,
And, often falling, climbs against the blast.
Low waves the rooted forest, vexed, and sheds
What of its tarnished honours yet remain—
Dashed down and scattered, by the tearing wind's
Assiduous fury, its gigantic limbs.
Thus struggling through the dissipated grove,
The whirling tempest raves along the plain;
And, on the cottage thatched or lordly roof
Keen-fastening, shakes them to the solid base.
Sleep frighted flies; and round the rocking dome,
For entrance eager, howls the savage blast.
Then too, they say, through all the burdened air
Long groans are heard, shrill sounds, and distant sighs,
That, uttered by the demon of the night,
Warn the devoted wretch of woe and death.

Huge uproar lords it wide. The clouds, commixed
With stars swift-gliding, sweep along the sky.
All Nature reels: till Nature's King, who oft
Amid tempestuous darkness dwells alone,
And on the wings of the careering wind
Walks dreadfully serene, commands a calm;
Then straight air, sea, and earth are hushed at once.

As yet 'tis midnight deep. The weary clouds,
Slow-meeting, mingle into solid gloom.
Now, while the drowsy world lies lost in sleep,
Let me associate with the serious Night,
And Contemplation, her sedate compeer;
Let me shake off the intrusive cares of day,
And lay the meddling senses all aside.

Where now, ye lying vanities of life!
Ye ever-tempting, ever-cheating train!
Where are you now? and what is your amount?
Vexation, disappointment, and remorse.
Sad, sickening thought! and yet deluded man,
A scene of crude disjointed visions past,
And broken slumbers, rises still resolved,
With new-flushed hopes, to run the giddy round.

Father of light and life! thou Good Supreme!
O teach me what is good! teach me Thyself!
Save me from folly, vanity, and vice,
From every low pursuit; and feed my soul
With knowledge, conscious peace, and virtue pure—
Sacred, substantial, never-fading bliss!

The keener tempests come: and, fuming dun
From all the livid east or piercing north,
Thick clouds ascend, in whose capacious womb
A vapoury deluge lies, to snow congealed.
Heavy they roll their fleecy world along,
And the sky saddens with the gathered storm.
Through the hushed air the whitening shower descends,
At first thin-wavering; till at last the flakes
Fall broad and wide and fast, dimming the day
With a continual flow. The cherished fields
Put on their winter-robe of purest white.
'Tis brightness all; save where the new snow melts
Along the mazy current. Low the woods
Bow their hoar head; and, ere the languid sun
Faint from the west emits his evening ray,
Earth's universal face, deep-hid and chill,
Is one wild dazzling waste, that buries wide
The works of man. Drooping, the labourer-ox
Stands covered o'er with snow, and then demands
The fruit of all his toil. The fowls of heaven,
Tamed by the cruel season, crowd around
The winnowing store, and claim the little boon
Which Providence assigns them. One alone,

The redbreast, sacred to the household gods,
Wisely regardful of the embroiling sky,
In joyless fields and thorny thickets leaves
His shivering mates, and pays to trusted man
His annual visit. Half afraid, he first
Against the window beats; then brisk alights
On the warm hearth; then, hopping o'er the floor,
Eyes all the smiling family askance,
And pecks, and starts, and wonders where he is—
Till, more familiar grown, the table-crumbs
Attract his slender feet. The foodless wilds
Pour forth their brown inhabitants. The hare,
Though timorous of heart, and hard beset
By death in various forms, dark snares, and dogs,
And more unpitying men, the garden seeks,
Urged on by fearless want. The bleating kind
Eye the bleak heaven, and next the glistening earth,
With looks of dumb despair; then, sad-dispersed,
Dig for the withered herb through heaps of snow.

Now, shepherds, to your helpless charge be kind:
Baffle the raging year, and fill their pens
With food at will; lodge them below the storm,
And watch them strict: for, from the bellowing east,
In this dire season, oft the whirlwind's wing
Sweeps up the burden of whole wintry plains
In one wide waft, and o'er the hapless flocks,
Hid in the hollow of two neighbouring hills,
The billowy tempest whelms; till, upward urged,
The valley to a shining mountain swells,
Tipt with a wreath high-curling in the sky.

As thus the snows arise, and, foul and fierce,
All Winter drives along the darkened air,
In his own loose-revolving fields the swain
Disastered stands; sees other hills ascend,
Of unknown joyless brow; and other scenes,
Of horrid prospect, shag the trackless plain;
Nor finds the river nor the forest, hid
Beneath the formless wild; but wanders on
From hill to dale, still more and more astray—
Impatient flouncing through the drifted heaps,
Stung with the thoughts of home: the thoughts of home
Rush on his nerves and call their vigour forth
In many a vain attempt. How sinks his soul!
What black despair, what horror fills his heart,
When, for the dusky spot which fancy feigned
His tufted cottage rising through the snow,

He meets the roughness of the middle waste,
Far from the track and blest abode of man;
While round him night resistless closes fast,
And every tempest, howling o'er his head,
Renders the savage wilderness more wild.
Then throng the busy shapes into his mind
Of covered pits, unfathomably deep,
A dire descent! beyond the power of frost;
Of faithless bogs; of precipices huge,
Smoothed up with snow; and (what is land unknown,
What water) of the still unfrozen spring,
In the loose marsh or solitary lake,
Where the fresh fountain from the bottom boils.
These check his fearful steps; and down he sinks
Beneath the shelter of the shapeless drift,
Thinking o'er all the bitterness of death,
Mixed with the tender anguish nature shoots
Through the wrung bosom of the dying man—
His wife, his children, and his friends unseen.
In vain for him the officious wife prepares
The fire fair-blazing and the vestment warm;
In vain his little children, peeping out
Into the mingling storm, demand their sire
With tears of artless innocence. Alas!
Nor wife nor children more shall he behold,
Nor friends, nor sacred home. On every nerve
The deadly Winter seizes, shuts up sense,
And, o'er his inmost vitals creeping cold,
Lays him along the snows a stiffened corse,
Stretched out, and bleaching in the northern blast.

Ah! little think the gay licentious proud,
Whom pleasure, power, and affluence surround—
They, who their thoughtless hours in giddy mirth,
And wanton, often cruel, riot waste—
Ah! little think they, while they dance along,
How many feel, this very moment, death
And all the sad variety of pain;
How many sink in the devouring flood,
Or more devouring flame; how many bleed,
By shameful variance betwixt man and man;
How many pine in want, and dungeon-glooms,
Shut from the common air and common use
Of their own limbs; how many drink the cup
Of baleful grief, or eat the bitter bread
Of misery; sore pierced by wintry winds,
How many shrink into the sordid hut
Of cheerless poverty; how many shake

With all the fiercer tortures of the mind,
Unbounded passion, madness, guilt, remorse—
Whence, tumbled headlong from the height of life,
They furnish matter for the tragic muse;
Even in the vale, where wisdom loves to dwell,
With friendship, peace, and contemplation joined,
How many, racked with honest passions, droop
In deep retired distress; how many stand
Around the death-bed of their dearest friends,
And point the parting anguish! Thought fond man
Of these, and all the thousand nameless ills
That one incessant struggle render life,
One scene of toil, of suffering, and of fate,
Vice in his high career would stand appalled,
And heedless rambling Impulse learn to think;
The conscious heart of Charity would warm,
And her wide wish Benevolence dilate;
The social tear would rise, the social sigh;
And, into clear perfection, gradual bliss,
Refining still, the social passions work.

And here can I forget the generous band
Who, touched with human woe, redressive searched
Into the horrors of the gloomy jail?
Unpitied and unheard where misery moans,
Where sickness pines, where thirst and hunger burn,
And poor misfortune feels the lash of vice;
While in the land of liberty-the land
Whose every street and public meeting glow
With open freedom-little tyrants raged,
Snatched the lean morsel from the starving mouth,
Tore from cold wintry limbs the tattered weed,
Even robbed them of the last of comforts, sleep,
The free-born Briton to the dungeon chained
Or, as the lust of cruelty prevailed,
At pleasure marked him with inglorious stripes,
And crushed out lives, by secret barbarous ways,
That for their country would have toiled or bled.
O great design! if executed well,
With patient care and wisdom-tempered zeal.
Ye sons of mercy! yet resume the search;
Drag forth the legal monsters into light,
Wrench from their hands Oppression's iron rod, 380
And bid the cruel feel the pains they give.
Much still untouched remains; in this rank age,
Much is the patriot's weeding hand required.
The toils of law-what dark insidious men
Have cumbrous added to perplex the truth

And lengthen simple justice into trade—
How glorious were the day that saw these broke,
And every man within the reach of right!

By wintry famine roused, from all the tract
Of horrid mountains which the shining Alps,
And wavy Apennines, and Pyrenees
Branch out stupendous into distant lands,
Cruel as death, and hungry as the grave!
Burning for blood, bony, and gaunt, and grim!
Assembling wolves in raging troops descend;
And, pouring o'er the country, bear along,
Keen as the north-wind sweeps the glossy snow.
All is their prize. They fasten on the steed,
Press him to earth, and pierce his mighty heart.
Nor can the bull his awful front defend,
Or shake the murdering savages away.
Rapacious, at the mother's throat they fly,
And tear the screaming infant from her breast.
The godlike face of man avails him naught.
Even Beauty, force divine! at whose bright glance
The generous lion stands in softened gaze,
Here bleeds, a hapless undistinguished prey.
But if, apprised of the severe attack,
The country be shut up, lured by the scent,
On churchyards drear (inhuman to relate!)
The disappointed prowlers fall, and dig
The shrouded body from the grave; o'er which,
Mixed with foul shades and frighted ghosts, they howl.

Among those hilly regions, where, embraced
In peaceful vales, the happy Grisons dwell,
Oft, rushing sudden from the loaded cliffs,
Mountains of snow their gathering terrors roll.
From steep to steep, loud thundering, down they come,
A wintry waste in dire commotion all;
And herds, and flocks, and travellers, and swains,
And sometimes whole brigades of marching troops,
Or hamlets sleeping in the dead of night,
Are deep beneath the smothering ruin whelmed.

Now, all amid the rigours of the year,
In the wild depth of winter, while without
The ceaseless winds blow ice, be my retreat,
Between the groaning forest and the shore,
Beat by the boundless multitude of waves,
A rural, sheltered, solitary scene;
Where ruddy fire and beaming tapers join

To cheer the gloom. There studious let me sit,
And hold high converse with the mighty dead—
Sages of ancient time, as gods revered,
As gods beneficent, who blessed mankind
With arts and arms, and humanized a world.
Roused at the inspiring thought, I throw aside
The long-lived volume, and deep-musing hail
The sacred shades that slowly rising pass
Before my wondering eyes. First Socrates,
Who, firmly good in a corrupted state,
Against the rage of tyrants single stood,
Invincible! calm reason's holy law,
That voice of God within the attentive mind,
Obeying, fearless or in life or death:
Great moral teacher! wisest of mankind!
Solon the next, who built his commonweal
On equity's wide base; by tender laws
A lively people curbing, yet undamped
Preserving still that quick peculiar fire,
Whence in the laurelled field of finer arts,
And of bold freedom, they unequalled shone,
The pride of smiling Greece and human-kind.
Lycurgus then, who bowed beneath the force
Of strictest discipline, severely wise,
All human passions. Following him I see,
As at Thermopylae he glorious fell,
The firm devoted chief, who proved by deeds
The hardest lesson which the other taught.
Then Aristides lifts his honest front;
Spotless of heart, to whom the unflattering voice
Of freedom gave the noblest name of Just;
In pure majestic poverty revered;
Who, even his glory to his country's weal
Submitting, swelled a haughty rival's fame.
Reared by his care, of softer ray appears
Cimon, sweet-souled; whose genius, rising strong,
Shook off the load of young debauch; abroad
The scourge of Persian pride, at home the friend
Of every worth and every splendid art;
Modest and simple in the pomp of wealth.
Then the last worthies of declining Greece,
Late-called to glory, in unequal times,
Pensive appear. The fair Corinthian boast,
Timoleon, tempered happy, mild, and firm,
Who wept the brother while the tyrant bled;
And, equal to the best, the Theban pair,
Whose virtues, in heroic concord joined,
Their country raised to freedom, empire, fame.

He too, with whom Athenian honour sunk,
And left a mass of sordid lees behind,—
Phocion the Good; in public life severe,
To virtue still inexorably firm;
But when, beneath his low illustrious roof,
Sweet peace and happy wisdom smoothed his brow,
Not friendship softer was, nor love more kind.
And he, the last of old Lycurgus' sons,
The generous victim to that vain attempt
To save a rotten state-Agis, who saw
Even Sparta's self to servile avarice sunk.
The two Achaian heroes close the train—
Aratus, who a while relumed the soul
Of fondly lingering liberty in Greece;
And he, her darling, as her latest hope,
The gallant Philopoemen, who to arms
Turned the luxurious pomp he could not cure,
Or toiling in his farm, a simple swain,
Or bold and skilful thundering in the field.

Of rougher front, a mighty people come,
A race of heroes! in those virtuous times
Which knew no stain, save that with partial flame
Their dearest country they too fondly loved.
Her better founder first, the Light of Rome,
Numa, who softened her rapacious sons;
Servius, the king who laid the solid base
On which o'er earth the vast republic spread.
Then the great consuls venerable rise:
The public father who the private quelled,
As on the dread tribunal, sternly sad;
He, whom his thankless country could not lose,
Camillus, only vengeful to her foes;
Fabricius, scorner of all-conquering gold,
And Cincinnatus, awful from the plough;
Thy willing victim, Carthage! bursting loose
From all that pleading Nature could oppose,
From a whole city's tears, by rigid faith
Imperious called, and honour's dire command;
Scipio, the gentle chief, humanely brave,
Who soon the race of spotless glory ran,
And, warm in youth, to the poetic shade
With friendship and philosophy retired;
Tully, whose powerful eloquence a while
Restrained the rapid fate of rushing Rome;
Unconquered Cato, virtuous in extreme;
And thou, unhappy Brutus, kind of heart,
Whose steady arm, by awful virtue urged,

Lifted the Roman steel against thy friend.
Thousands besides the tribute of a verse
Demand; but who can count the stars of heaven?
Who sing their influence on this lower world?

Behold, who yonder comes! in sober state,
Fair, mild, and strong as is a vernal sun:
'Tis Phoebus' self, or else the Mantuan swain!
Great Homer too appears, of daring wing,
Parent of song! and equal by his side,
The British Muse; join'd hand in hand they walk,
Darkling, full up the middle steep to fame.
Nor absent are those shades, whose skilful touch
Pathetic drew the impassioned heart, and charmed
Transported Athens with the moral scene;
Nor those who, tuneful, waked the enchanting lyre.

First of your kind! society divine!
Still visit thus my nights, for you reserved,
And mount my soaring soul to thoughts like yours.
Silence, thou lonely power! the door be thine;
See on the hallowed hour that none intrude,
Save a few chosen friends, who sometimes deign
To bless my humble roof, with sense refined,
Learning digested well, exalted faith,
Unstudied wit, and humour ever gay.
Or from the Muses' hill will Pope descend,
To raise the sacred hour, to bid it smile,
And with the social spirit warm the heart;
For, though not sweeter his own Homer sings,
Yet is his life the more endearing song.

Where art thou, Hammond? thou the darling pride,
The friend and lover of the tuneful throng!
Ah! why, dear youth, in all the blooming prime
Of vernal genius, where, disclosing fast,
Each active worth, each manly virtue lay,
Why wert thou ravished from our hope so soon?
What now avails that noble thirst of fame,
Which stung thy fervent breast? that treasured store
Of knowledge, early gained? that eager zeal
To serve thy country, glowing in the band
Of youthful patriots who sustain her name?
What now, alas! that life-diffusing charm
Of sprightly wit? that rapture for the muse,
That heart of friendship, and that soul of joy,
Which bade with softest light thy virtues smile?
Ah! only showed to check our fond pursuits,

And teach our humbled hopes that life is vain.

Thus in some deep retirement would I pass
The winter-glooms with friends of pliant soul,
Or blithe or solemn, as the theme inspired:
With them would search if nature's boundless frame
Was called, late-rising, from the void of night,
Or sprung eternal from the Eternal Mind;
Its life, its laws, its progress, and its end.
Hence larger prospects of the beauteous whole
Would gradual open on our opening minds;
And each diffusive harmony unite
In full perfection to the astonished eye.
Then would we try to scan the moral world,
Which, though to us it seems embroiled, moves on
In higher order, fitted and impelled
By wisdom's finest hand, and issuing all
In general good. The sage historic muse
Should next conduct us through the deeps of time,
Show us how empire grew, declined, and fell
In scattered states; what makes the nations smile,
Improves their soil, and gives them double suns;
And why they pine beneath the brightest skies
In nature's richest lap. As thus we talked,
Our hearts would burn within us, would inhale
That portion of divinity, that ray
Of purest heaven, which lights the public soul
Of patriots and of heroes. But, if doomed
In powerless humble fortune to repress
These ardent risings of the kindling soul,
Then, even superior to ambition, we
Would learn the private virtues-how to glide
Through shades and plains along the smoothest stream
Of rural life: or, snatched away by hope
Through the dim spaces of futurity,
With earnest eye anticipate those scenes
Of happiness and wonder, where the mind,
In endless growth and infinite ascent,
Rises from state to state, and world to world.
But, when with these the serious thought is foiled,
We, shifting for relief, would play the shapes
Of frolic fancy; and incessant form
Those rapid pictures, that assembled train
Of fleet ideas, never joined before,
Whence lively wit excites to gay surprise,
Or folly-painting humour, grave himself,
Calls laughter forth, deep-shaking every nerve.

Meantime the village rouses up the fire;
While, well attested, and as well believed,
Heard solemn, goes the goblin-story round,
Till superstitious horror creeps o'er all.
Or frequent in the sounding hall they wake
The rural gambol. Rustic mirth goes round—
The simple joke that takes the shepherd's heart,
Easily pleased; the long loud laugh sincere;
The kiss, snatched hasty from the sidelong maid
On purpose guardless, or pretending sleep;
The leap, the slap, the haul; and, shook to notes
Of native music, the respondent dance.
Thus jocund fleets with them the winter-night.

The city swarms intense. The public haunt,
Full of each theme and warm with mixed discourse,
Hums indistinct. The sons of riot flow
Down the loose stream of false enchanted joy
To swift destruction. On the rankled soul
The gaming fury falls; and in one gulf
Of total ruin, honour, virtue, peace,
Friends, families, and fortune headlong sink.
Up springs the dance along the lighted dome,
Mixed and evolved a thousand sprightly ways.
The glittering court effuses every pomp;
The circle deepens; beamed from gaudy robes,
Tapers, and sparkling gems, and radiant eyes,
A soft effulgence o'er the palace waves
While, a gay insect in his summer shine,
The fop, light-fluttering, spreads his mealy wings.

Dread o'er the scene the ghost of Hamlet stalks;
Othello rages; poor Monimia mourns;
And Belvidera pours her soul in love.
Terror alarms the breast; the comely tear
Steals o'er the cheek: or else the comic muse
Holds to the world a picture of itself,
And raises sly the fair impartial laugh.
Sometimes she lifts her strain, and paints the scenes
Of beauteous life-whate'er can deck mankind,
Or charm the heart, in generous Bevil showed.

O thou, whose wisdom, solid yet refined,
Whose patriot virtues, and consummate skill
To touch the finer springs that move the world,
Joined to whate' er the graces can bestow,
And all Apollo's animating fire
Give thee with pleasing dignity to shine

At once the guardian, ornament, and joy
Of polished life—permit the rural muse,
O Chesterfield, to grace with thee her song.
Ere to the shades again she humbly flies,
Indulge her fond ambition, in thy train
(For every muse has in thy train a place)
To mark thy various full-accomplished mind—
To mark that spirit which with British scorn
Rejects the allurements of corrupted power;
That elegant politeness which excels,
Even in the judgement of presumptuous France,
The boasted manners of her shining court;
That wit, the vivid energy of sense,
The truth of nature, which with Attic point,
And kind well-tempered satire, smoothly keen,
Steals through the soul and without pain corrects.
Or, rising thence with yet a brighter flame,
O let me hail thee on some glorious day,
When to the listening senate ardent crowd
Britannia's sons to hear her pleaded cause!
Then, dressed by thee, more amiably fair,
Truth the soft robe of mild persuasion wears;
Thou to assenting reason giv'st again
Her own enlightened thoughts; called from the heart,
The obedient passions on thy voice attend;
And even reluctant party feels a while
Thy gracious power, as through the varied maze
Of eloquence, now smooth, now quick, now strong,
Profound and clear, you roll the copious flood.

To thy loved haunt return, my happy muse:
For now, behold! the joyous Winter days,
Frosty, succeed; and through the blue serene,
For sight too fine, the ethereal nitre flies,
Killing infectious damps, and the spent air
Storing afresh with elemental life.
Close crowds the shining atmosphere; and binds
Our strengthened bodies in its cold embrace,
Constringent; feeds, and animates our blood;
Refines our spirits, through the new-strung nerves
In swifter sallies darting to the brain—
Where sits the soul, intense, collected, cool,
Bright as the skies, and as the season keen.
All nature feels the renovating force
Of Winter—only to the thoughtless eye
In ruin seen. The frost-concocted glebe
Draws in abundant vegetable soul,
And gathers vigour for the coming year;

A stronger glow sits on the lively cheek
Of ruddy fire; and luculent along
The purer rivers flow: their sullen deeps,
Transparent, open to the shepherd's gaze,
And murmur hoarser at the fixing frost.

What art thou, frost? and whence are thy keen stores
Derived, thou secret all-invading power,
Whom even the illusive fluid cannot fly?
Is not thy potent energy, unseen,
Myriads of little salts, or hooked, or shaped
Like double wedges, and diffused immense
Through water, earth, and ether? Hence at eve,
Steamed eager from the red horizon round,
With the fierce rage of Winter deep suffused,
An icy gale, oft shifting, o'er the pool
Breathes a blue film, and in its mid-career
Arrests the bickering stream. The loosened ice,
Let down the flood and half dissolved by day,
Rustles no more; but to the sedgy bank
Fast grows, or gathers round the pointed stone,
A crystal pavement, by the breath of heaven
Cemented firm; till, seized from shore to shore,
The whole imprisoned river growls below.
Loud rings the frozen earth, and hard reflects
A double noise; while, at his evening watch,
The village-dog deters the nightly thief;
The heifer lows; the distant waterfall
Swells in the breeze; and with the hasty tread
Of traveller the hollow-sounding plain
Shakes from afar. The full ethereal round,
Infinite worlds disclosing to the view,
Shines out intensely keen, and, all one cope
Of starry glitter, glows from pole to pole.
From pole to pole the rigid influence falls
Through the still night incessant, heavy, strong,
And seizes nature fast. It freezes on,
Till morn, late-rising o'er the drooping world,
Lifts her pale eye unjoyous. Then appears
The various labour of the silent night—
Prone from the dripping eave, and dumb cascade,
Whose idle torrents only seem to roar,
The pendent icicle; the frost-work fair,
Where transient hues and fancied figures rise;
Wide-spouted o'er the hill the frozen brook,
A livid tract, cold-gleaming on the morn;
The forest bent beneath the plumy wave;
And by the frost refined the whiter snow

Incrusted hard, and sounding to the tread
Of early shepherd, as he pensive seeks
His pining flock, or from the mountain top,
Pleased with the slippery surface, swift descends.

On blithesome frolics bent, the youthful swains,
While every work of man is laid at rest,
Fond o'er the river crowd, in various sport
And revelry dissolved; where, mixing glad,
Happiest of all the train! the raptured boy
Lashes the whirling top. Or, where the Rhine
Branched out in many a long canal extends,
From every province swarming, void of care,
Batavia rushes forth; and, as they sweep
On sounding skates a thousand different ways
In circling poise swift as the winds along,
The then gay land is maddened all to joy.
Nor less the northern courts, wide o'er the snow,
Pour a new pomp. Eager, on rapid sleds,
Their vigorous youth in bold contention wheel
The long-resounding course. Meantime, to raise
The manly strife, with highly blooming charms,
Flushed by the season, Scandinavia's dames
Or Russia's buxom daughters glow around.

Pure, quick, and sportful is the wholesome day;
But soon elapsed. The horizontal sun
Broad o'er the south hangs at his utmost noon;
And ineffectual strikes the gelid cliff.
His azure gloss the mountain still maintains,
Nor feels the feeble touch. Perhaps the vale
Relents awhile to the reflected ray;
Or from the forest falls the clustered snow,
Myriads of gems, that in the waving gleam
Gay-twinkle as they scatter. Thick around
Thunders the sport of those who with the gun,
And dog impatient bounding at the shot,
Worse than the season desolate the fields,
And, adding to the ruins of the year,
Distress the footed or the feathered game.

But what is this? Our infant Winter sinks
Divested of his grandeur should our eye
Astonished shoot into the frigid zone,
Where for relentless months continual night
Holds o'er the glittering waste her starry reign.
There, through the prison of unbounded wilds,
Barred by the hand of nature from escape,

Wide roams the Russian exile. Naught around
Strikes his sad eye but deserts lost in snow,
And heavy-loaded groves, and solid floods
That stretch athwart the solitary vast
Their icy horrors to the frozen main,
And cheerless towns far distant-never blessed,
Save when its annual course the caravan
Bends to the golden coast of rich Cathay,
With news of human-kind. Yet there life glows;
Yet, cherished there, beneath the shining waste
The furry nations harbour-tipt with jet,
Fair ermines spotless as the snows they press;
Sables of glossy black; and, dark-embrowned,
Or beauteous freakt with many a mingled hue,
Thousands besides, the costly pride of courts.
There, warm together pressed, the trooping deer
Sleep on the new-fallen snows; and, scarce his head
Raised o'er the heapy wreath, the branching elk
Lies slumbering sullen in the white abyss.
The ruthless hunter wants nor dogs nor toils,
Nor with the dread of sounding bows he drives
The fearful flying race-with ponderous clubs,
As weak against the mountain-heaps they push
Their beating breast in vain, and piteous bray,
He lays them quivering on the ensanguined snows,
And with loud shouts rejoicing bears them home.
There, through the piny forest half-absorpt,
Rough tenant of these shades, the shapeless bear,
With dangling ice all horrid, stalks forlorn;
Slow-paced, and sourer as the storms increase,
He makes his bed beneath the inclement drift,
And, with stern patience, scorning weak complaint,
Hardens his heart against assailing want.

Wide o'er the spacious regions of the north,
That see Bootes urge his tardy wain,
A boisterous race, by frosty Caurus pierced,
Who little pleasure know and fear no pain,
Prolific swarm. They once relumed the flame
Of lost mankind in polished slavery sunk;
Drove martial horde on horde, with dreadful sweep
Resistless rushing o'er the enfeebled south,
And gave the vanquished world another form.
Not such the sons of Lapland: wisely they
Despise the insensate barbarous trade of war;
They ask no more than simple Nature gives;
They love their mountains and enjoy their storms.
No false desires, no pride-created wants,

Disturb the peaceful current of their time,
And through the restless ever-tortured maze
Of pleasure or ambition bid it rage.
Their reindeer form their riches. These their tents,
Their robes, their beds, and all their homely wealth
Supply, their wholesome fare, and cheerful cups.
Obsequious at their call, the docile tribe
Yield to the sled their necks, and whirl them swift
O'er hill and dale, heaped into one expanse
Of marbled snow, or, far as eye can sweep,
With a blue crust of ice unbounded glazed.
By dancing meteors then, that ceaseless shake
A waving blaze refracted o'er the heavens,
And vivid moons, and stars that keener play
With doubled lustre from the radiant waste,
Even in the depth of polar night they find
A wondrous day-enough to light the chase
Or guide their daring steps to Finland fairs.
Wished spring returns; and from the hazy south,
While dim Aurora slowly moves before,
The welcome sun, just verging up at first,
By small degrees extends the swelling curve;
Till, seen at last for gay rejoicing months,
Still round and round his spiral course he winds,
And, as he nearly dips his flaming orb,
Wheels up again and re-ascends the sky.
In that glad season, from the lakes and floods,
Where pure Niemi's fairy mountains rise,
And fringed with roses Tenglio rolls his stream,
They draw the copious fry. With these at eve
They cheerful-loaded to their tents repair,
Where, all day long in useful cares employed,
Their kind unblemished wives the fire prepare.
Thrice happy race! by poverty secured
From legal plunder and rapacious power,
In whom fell interest never yet has sown
The seeds of vice, whose spotless swains ne'er knew
Injurious deed, nor, blasted by the breath
Of faithless love, their blooming daughters woe.

Still pressing on, beyond Tornea's lake,
And Hecla flaming through a waste of snow,
And farthest Greenland, to the pole itself,
Where, failing gradual, life at length goes out,
The muse expands her solitary flight;
And, hovering o'er the wild stupendous scene;
Beholds new seas beneath another sky.
Throned in his palace of cerulean ice,

Here Winter holds his unrejoicing court;
And through his airy hall the loud misrule
Of driving tempest is for ever heard:
Here the grim tyrant meditates his wrath;
Here arms his winds with all-subduing frost;
Moulds his fierce hail, and treasures up his snows,
With which he now oppresses half the globe.

Thence winding eastward to the Tartar's coast,
She sweeps the howling margin of the main;
Where, undissolving from the first of time,
Snows swell on snows amazing to the sky;
And icy mountains high on mountains piled
Seem to the shivering sailor from afar,
Shapeless and white, an atmosphere of clouds.
Projected huge and horrid o'er the surge,
Alps frown on Alps; or, rushing hideous down,
As if old Chaos was again returned,
Wide-rend the deep and shake the solid pole.
Ocean itself no longer can resist
The binding fury; but, in all its rage
Of tempest taken by the boundless frost,
Is many a fathom to the bottom chained,
And bid to roar no more-a bleak expanse
Shagged o'er with wavy rocks, cheerless, and void
Of every life, that from the dreary months
Flies conscious southward. Miserable they!
Who, here entangled in the gathering ice,
Take their last look of the descending sun;
While, full of death and fierce with tenfold frost,
The long long night, incumbent o'er their heads,
Falls horrible! Such was the Briton's fate,
As with first prow (what have not Britons dared?)
He for the passage sought, attempted since
So much in vain, and seeming to be shut
By jealous nature with eternal bars.
In these fell regions, in Arzina caught,
And to the stony deep his idle ship
Immediate sealed, he with his hapless crew,
Each full exerted at his several task,
Froze into statues-to the cordage glued
The sailor, and the pilot to the helm.

Hard by these shores, where scarce his freezing stream
Rolls the wild Oby, live the last of men;
And, half enlivened by the distant sun,
That rears and ripens man as well as plants,
Here human nature wears its rudest form.

Deep from the piercing Season sunk in caves,
Here by dull fires and with unjoyous cheer
They waste the tedious gloom: immersed in furs
Doze the gross race-nor sprightly jest, nor song,
Nor tenderness they know, nor aught of life
Beyond the kindred bears that stalk without—
Till Morn at length, her roses drooping all,
Sheds a long twilight brightening o'er their fields
And calls the quivered savage to the chase.

What cannot active government perform,
New-moulding man? Wide-stretching from these shores,
A people savage from remotest time,
A huge neglected empire, one vast mind
By heaven inspired from Gothic darkness called.
Immortal Peter! first of monarchs! He
His stubborn country tamed,-her rocks, her fens,
Her floods, her seas, her ill-submitting sons;
And, while the fierce barbarian he subdued,
To more exalted soul he raised the man.
Ye shades of ancient heroes, ye who toiled
Through long successive ages to build up
A labouring plan of state, behold at once
The wonder done! behold the matchless prince!
Who left his native throne, where reigned till then
A mighty shadow of unreal power;
Who greatly spurned the slothful pomp of courts;
And, roaming every land, in every port
His sceptre laid aside, with glorious hand
Unwearied plying the mechanic tool,
Gathered the seeds of trade, of useful arts,
Of civil wisdom, and of martial skill.
Charged with the stores of Europe home he goes!
Then cities rise amid the illumined waste;
O'er joyless deserts smiles the rural reign;
Far-distant flood to flood is social joined;
The astonished Euxine hears the Baltic roar;
Proud navies ride on seas that never foamed
With daring keel before; and armies stretch
Each way their dazzling files, repressing here
The frantic Alexander of the north,
And awing there stern Othman's shrinking sons.
Sloth flies the land, and ignorance and vice,
Of old dishonour proud: it glows around,
Taught by the royal hand that roused the whole,
One scene of arts, of arms, of rising trade—
For, what his wisdom planned and power enforced,
More potent still his great example showed.

Muttering, the winds at eve with blunted point
Blow hollow-blustering from the south. Subdued,
The frost resolves into a trickling thaw.
Spotted the mountains shine: loose sleet descends,
And floods the country round. The rivers swell,
Of bonds impatient. Sudden from the hills,
O'er rocks and woods, in broad brown cataracts,
A thousand snow-fed torrents shoot at once;
And, where they rush, the wide-resounding plain
Is left one slimy waste. Those sullen seas,
That wash'd the ungenial pole, will rest no more
Beneath the shackles of the mighty north,
But, rousing all their waves, resistless heave.
And, hark! the lengthening roar continuous runs
Athwart the rifted deep: at once it bursts,
And piles a thousand mountains to the clouds.
Ill fares the bark, with trembling wretches charged,
That, tossed amid the floating fragments, moors
Beneath the shelter of an icy isle,
While night o'erwhelms the sea, and horror looks
More horrible. Can human force endure
The assembled mischiefs that besiege them round?—
Heart-gnawing hunger, fainting weariness,
The roar of winds and waves, the crush of ice,
Now ceasing, now renewed with louder rage,
And in dire echoes bellowing round the main.
More to embroil the deep, Leviathan
And his unwieldy train in dreadful sport
Tempest the loosened brine; while through the gloom
Far from the bleak inhospitable shore,
Loading the winds, is heard the hungry howl
Of famished monsters, there awaiting wrecks.
Yet Providence, that ever-waking Eye,
Looks down with pity on the feeble toil
Of mortals lost to hope, and lights them safe
Through all this dreary labyrinth of fate.

'Tis done! Dread Winter spreads his latest glooms,
And reigns tremendous o'er the conquered year.
How dead the vegetable kingdom lies!
How dumb the tuneful! Horror wide extends
His desolate domain. Behold, fond man!
See here thy pictured life; pass some few years,
Thy flowering Spring, thy Summer's ardent strength,
Thy sober Autumn fading into age,
And pale concluding Winter comes at last
And shuts the scene. Ah! whither now are fled

Those dreams of greatness? those unsolid hopes
Of happiness? those longings after fame?
Those restless cares? those busy bustling days?
Those gay-spent festive nights? those veering thoughts,
Lost between good and ill, that shared thy life?
All now are vanished! Virtue sole survives—
Immortal, never-failing friend of man,
His guide to happiness on high. And see!
'Tis come, the glorious morn! the second birth
Of heaven and earth! awakening nature hears
The new-creating word, and starts to life
In every heightened form, from pain and death
For ever free. The great eternal scheme,
Involving all, and in a perfect whole
Uniting, as the prospect wider spreads,
To reason's eye refined clears up apace.
Ye vainly wise! ye blind presumptuous! now,
Confounded in the dust, adore that Power
And Wisdom-oft arraigned: see now the cause
Why unassuming worth in secret lived
And died neglected: why the good man's share
In life was gall and bitterness of soul:
Why the lone widow and her orphans pined
In starving solitude; while luxury
In palaces lay straining her low thought
To form unreal wants: why heaven-born truth
And moderation fair wore the red marks
Of superstition's scourge; why licensed pain,
That cruel spoiler, that embosomed foe,
Embittered all our bliss. Ye good distressed!
Ye noble few! who here unbending stand
Beneath life's pressure, yet bear up a while,
And what your bounded view, which only saw
A little part, deemed evil is no more:
The storms of wintry time will quickly pass,
And one unbounded Spring encircle all.

WINTER: A PREFACE (for the second edition)

The following Preface by Thomson was written for the second edition of Winter, and continued to be printed with separate editions of that poem; but was dropped in 1730, when the first collected edition of The Seasons appeared; it constitutes Thomson's apology for poesy, or rather his vindication of poetry;—

I am neither ignorant nor concerned how much one may suffer in the opinion of several persons of great gravity and character by the study and pursuit of poetry. Although there may seem to be Some appearance of reason for the present contempt of it as managed by the most part of our modern writers, yet that any man should seriously declare against that divine art is really amazing. It is declaring against the most charming power of imagination, the most exalting force of thought, the most affecting touch of sentiment—in a word, against the very soul of all learning and politeness. It is affronting the universal taste of mankind, and declaring against what has charmed the listening world from Moses down to Milton. In fine, it is even declaring against the sublimest passages of the inspired writings themselves, and what seems to be the peculiar language of heaven.

The truth of the case is this; These weak-sighted gentlemen cannot bear the strong light of poetry and the finer and more amusing scene of things it displays. But must those therefore whom heaven has blessed with the discerning eye shut it to keep them company?

It is pleasant enough, however, to observe frequently in these enemies of poetry an awkward imitation of it. They sometimes have their little brightnesses when the opening glooms will permit. Nay, I have seen their heaviness on some occasions deign to turn friskish, and witty, in which they make just such another figure as Aesop's Ass when he began to fawn. To complete the absurdity, they would even in their efforts against Poetry fain be poetical; like those gentlemen that reason with a great deal of zeal and severity against reason.

That there are frequent and notorious abuses of Poetry is as true as that the best things are most liable to that misfortune; but is there no end of that clamorous argument against the use of things from the abuse of them? and yet, I hope, that no man who has the least sense of shame in him will fall into it after the present sulphureous attacker of the stage.

To insist no further on this head, let poetry once more be restored to her ancient truth and purity; let her be inspired from heaven, and in return her incense ascend thither; let her exchange her low, venal, trifling, subjects for such as are fair, useful, and magnificent; and let her execute these so as at once to please, instruct, surprise, and astonish: and then of necessity the most inveterate ignorance, and prejudice, shall be struck dumb; and poets yet become the delight and wonder of mankind.

But this happy period is not to be expected, till some longwished, illustrious man of equal power and beneficence rise on the wintry world of letters: one of a genuine and unbounded greatness and generosity of mind; who, far above all the pomp and pride of fortune, scorns the little addressful flatterer; pierces through the disguised designing villain; discountenances all the reigning fopperies of a tasteless age: and who, stretching his views into late futurity, has the true interest of virtue, learning, and mankind entirely at heart-a character so nobly desirable that to an honest heart it is almost incredible so few should have the ambition to deserve it.

Nothing can have a better influence towards the revival of poetry than the choosing of great and serious subjects, such as at once amuse the fancy, enlighten the head, and warm the heart. These give a weight and dignity to the poem; nor is the pleasure—I should say rapture—both the writer and the reader feels unwarranted by reason or followed by repentant disgust. To be able to write on a dry, barren theme is looked upon by some as the sign of a happy, fruitful genius:-fruitful indeed! like one of the pendant gardens in Cheapside, watered every morning by the hand of the Alderman himself. And what are we commonly entertained with on these occasions save forced unaffecting fancies, little glittering prettinesses, mixed turns of wit and expression, which are as widely different from native poetry as buffoonery is from the perfection of human thinking? A genius fired with the charms of truth and nature is tuned to a sublimer pitch, and scorns to associate with such subjects.

I cannot more emphatically recommend this poetical ambition than by the four following lines from Mr. Hill's poem, called The Judgment Day, which is so singular an instance of it:—

For me, suffice it to have taught my Muse,
The tuneful Triflings of her tribe to shun;
And rais'd her warmth such heavenly themes to chuse,
As, in past ages, the best garlands won.

I know no subject more elevating, more amusing; more ready to awake the poetical enthusiasm, the philosophical reflection, and the moral sentiment, than the works of Nature. Where can we meet with such variety, such beauty, such magnificence? All that enlarges and transports the soul! What more inspiring than a calm, wide survey of them? In every dress nature is greatly charming-whether she puts on the crimson robes of the morning, the strong effulgence of noon, the sober suit of the evening, or the deep sables of blackness and tempest! How gay looks the Spring! how glorious the Summer! How pleasing the Autumn! and how venerable the Winter!-But there is no thinking of these things without breaking out into poetry; which is, by-the by, a plain and undeniable argument of their superior excellence. For this reason the best, both ancient, and modern, Poets have been passionately fond of retirement, and solitude. The wild romantic country was their delight. And they seem never to have been more happy, than when, lost in unfrequented fields, far from the little busy world, they were at leisure, to meditate, and sing the Works of Nature.

The book of Job, that noble and ancient poem, which, even, strikes so forcibly through a mangling translation, is crowned with a description of the grand works of Nature; and that, too, from the mouth of their Almighty Author.

It was this devotion to the works of Nature that, in his Georgics, inspired the rural Virgil to write so inimitably; and who can forbear joining with him in this declaration of his, which has been the rapture of ages?

Me vero primum dulces ante omnia Musae,
Quarum sacra fero ingenti perculsus amore,
Accipiant; caelique vias et sidera monstrent,
Defectus solis varios, lunaeque labores:
Unde tremor terris: qua vi maria alta tumescant
Obicibus ruptis, rursusque in seipsa residant:
Quid tantum oceano properent se tingere soles
Hyberni: vel quae tardis mora noctibus obstet.
Sin, has ne possim naturae accedere partes,
Frigidus obstiterit circum praecordia sanguis;
Rura mihi et rigui placeant in valli bus amnes,
Flumina amem silvasque inglorius.

Which may be Englished thus:—

Me may the Muses, my supreme delight!
Whose priest I am, smit with immense desire,
Snatch to their care; the starry tracts disclose,

The sun's distress, the labours of the moon:
Whence the earth quakes: and by what force the deeps
Heave at the rocks, then on themselves reflow:
Why winter-suns to plunge in ocean speed:
And what retards the lazy summer-night.
But, lest I should these mystic-truths attain,
If the cold current freezes round my heart,
The country me, the brooky vales may please
Mid woods and streams unknown.

I cannot put an end to this Preface without taking the freedom to offer my most sincere and grateful acknowledgments to all those gentlemen who have given my first performance so favourable a reception.

It is with the blest pleasure, and a rising ambition, that I reflect on the honour Mr. Hill has done me in recommending my poem to the world after a manner so peculiar to himself-than whom none approves and obliges with a nobler and more unreserving promptitude of soul. His favours are the very smiles of humanity, graceful and easy, flowing from and to the heart. This agreeable train of thought awakens naturally in my mind all the other parts of his great and amiable character, which I know not well how to quit, and yet dare not here pursue. Every reader who has a heart to be moved must feel the most gentle power of poetry in the lines with which Mira has graced my poem.

It perhaps might be reckoned vanity in me to say how richly I value the approbation of a gentleman of Mr. Malloch's fine and exact taste, so justly dear and valuable to all those that have the happiness of knowing him, and who-to say no more of him-will abundantly make good to the world the early promise his admired piece of William and Margaret has given. I only wish my description of the various appearance of nature in Winter (and, as I purpose, in the other Seasons) may have the good fortune to give the reader some of that true pleasure which they, in their agreeable succession, are always sure to inspire into my heart.

A HYMN ON THE SEASONS

These, as they change, Almighty Father! these
Are but the varied God. The rolling year
Is full of thee. Forth in the pleasing Spring
Thy beauty walks, thy tenderness and love.
Wide flush the fields; the softening air is balm;
Echo the mountains round; the forest smiles;
And every sense, and every heart, is joy.
Then comes thy glory in the Summer-months,
With light and heat refulgent. Then thy sun
Shoots full perfection through the swelling year:
And oft thy voice in dreadful thunder speaks,
And oft, at dawn, deep noon, or falling eve,
By brooks and groves, in hollow-whispering gales.
Thy bounty shines in Autumn unconfined,
And spreads a common feast for all that lives.

In Winter awful thou! with clouds and storms
Around thee thrown, tempest o'er tempest rolled,
Majestic darkness! On the whirlwind's wing
Riding sublime, thou bidst the world adore,
And humblest nature with thy northern blast.

Mysterious round! what skill, what force divine,
Deep-felt in these appear! a simple train,
Yet so delightful mixed, with such kind art,
Such beauty and beneficence combined,
Shade unperceived so softening into shade,
And all so forming an harmonious whole
That, as they still succeed, they ravish still.
But, wandering oft with brute unconscious gaze,
Man marks not thee, marks not the mighty hand
That, ever busy, wheels the silent spheres,
Works in the secret deep, shoots steaming thence
The fair profusion that o'erspreads the Spring,
Flings from the sun direct the flaming day,
Feeds every creature, hurls the tempest forth,
And, as on earth this grateful change revolves,
With transport touches all the springs of life.

Nature, attend! join, every living soul
Beneath the spacious temple of the sky,
In adoration join; and ardent raise
One general song! To him, ye vocal gales,
Breathe soft, whose spirit in your freshness breathes:
Oh! talk of him in solitary glooms,
Where, o'er the rock, the scarcely-waving pine
Fills the brown shade with a religious awe.
And ye, whose bolder note is heard afar,
Who shake the astonished world, lift high to Heaven
The impetuous song, and say from whom you rage.
His praise, ye brooks, attune, ye trembling rills;
And let me catch it as I muse along.
Ye headlong torrents, rapid and profound;
Ye softer floods, that lead the humid maze
Along the vale; and thou, majestic main,
A secret world of wonders in thyself,
Sound his stupendous praise, whose greater voice
Or bids you roar or bids your roarings fall.
Soft roll your incense, herbs, and fruits, and flowers,
In mingled clouds to him, whose sun exalts,
Whose breath perfumes you, and whose pencil paints.
Ye forests, bend; ye harvests, wave to him—
Breathe your still song into the reaper's heart
As home he goes beneath the joyous moon.

Ye that keep watch in heaven, as earth asleep
Unconscious lies, effuse your mildest beams,
Ye constellations! while your angels strike
Amid the spangled sky the silver lyre.
Great source of day! best image here below
Of thy Creator, ever pouring wide
From world to world the vital ocean round!
On nature write with every beam his praise.
The thunder rolls: be hushed the prostrate world,
While cloud to cloud returns the solemn hymn.
Bleat out afresh, ye hills; ye mossy rocks,
Retain the sound; the broad responsive low,
Ye valleys, raise; for the Great Shepherd reigns,
And his unsuffering kingdom yet will come.
Ye woodlands all, awake: a boundless song
Burst from the groves; and, when the restless day,
Expiring, lays the warbling world asleep,
Sweetest of birds, sweet Philomela! charm
The listening shades, and teach the night his praise!
Ye, chief, for whom the whole creation smiles,
At once the head, the heart, the tongue of all,
Crown the great hymn! In swarming cities vast,
Assembled men, to the deep organ join
The long-resounding voice, oft breaking clear
At solemn pauses through the swelling bass;
And, as each mingling flame increases each,
In one united ardour rise to heaven.
Or, if you rather choose the rural shade,
And find a fane in every sacred grove,
There let the shepherd's flute, the virgin's lay,
The prompting seraph, and the poet's lyre
Still sing the God of Seasons as they roll,
For me, when I forget the darling theme,
Whether the blossom blows, the summer-ray
Russets the plain, inspiring autumn gleams,
Or winter rises in the blackening east,
Be my tongue mute, may fancy paint no more,
And, dead to joy, forget my heart to beat!

Should fate command me to the farthest verge
Of the green earth, to distant barbarous climes,
Rivers unknown to song, where first the sun
Gilds Indian mountains, or his setting beam
Flames on the Atlantic isles, 'tis nought to me;
Since God is ever present, ever felt,
In the void waste as in the city full,
And where he vital spreads there must be joy.
When even at last the solemn hour shall come,

And wing my mystic flight to future worlds,
I cheerful will obey; there, with new powers, no
Will rising wonders sing: I cannot go
Where universal love not smiles around,
Sustaining all yon orbs and all their sons;
From seeming evil still educing good,
And better thence again, and better still,
In infinite progression. But I lose
Myself in him, in light ineffable!
Come then, expressive Silence, muse his praise.

A CHRONOLOGY

TO ELUCIDATE AND ILLUSTRATE THE LIFE AND TIMES OF JAMES THOMSON

1666. Birth of Thomas Thomson, the poet's father. Minister of Ednam, Roxburghshire. 1693. Marries Beatrix, daughter of Alexander Trotter, of Widehope (a small lairdship in Roxburghshire).

1694. Birth of Voltaire.

1700. Birth, at Ednam or Widehope, of James Thomson, the poet—fourth child (third son) of his parents; born (probably) on the 7th, baptized on the 15th of September. In the November following, his father inducted into the parish of Southdean, Roxburghshire. Birth of David Malloch (or Mallet). Death of Dryden.

1709. Birth of Johnson. 1712. Young Thomson attends a Grammar School in Jedburgh, some eight miles or so from Southdean. His acquaintance with Mr. (afterwards the Rev.) Robert Riccaltoun, farmer at Earlshaugh, begins about this time. First attempts at versifying, a year or two later.

1715. Young Thomson enters Edinburgh University.

1716. Death of his father, in February, while exorcizing a ghost. Home transferred to Edinburgh.

1719. Death of Addison.

1720. Thomson now a student of Divinity. Continues versifying, chiefly on rural subjects in the heroic couplet; contributes to The Edinburgh Miscellany Of a Country Life, &c.

1721. Birth of Collins. Walpole Prime Minister (till 1742).

1724. Thomson still at the University. Adverse criticism, by the Professor of Divinity, of one of his college exercises (a discourse on the 10th portion of Psalm cxix), the turning-point of his life.

1725. End of February, Thomson sets out to seek his fortune in London: embarks at Leith, not again to see Scotland. Visits Drury Lane Theatre, and sees Gato acted. Death of his mother, in May. In July, acting as tutor to Lord Binning's son, at Barnet, near London. Composition of Winter in the following autumn and winter. Publication of Allan Ramsay's The Gentle Shepherd.

1726. I March, Winter, a thin folio of 16 pp., 40511., price 18., John Millan, publisher. Dyer's Grongar Hill published. Thomson acting as tutor in an academy in London. Acquaintance with Aaron Hill. Second edition of Winter, in June.

1727. Death of Sir Isaac Newton: in June, Thomson publishes a poem To the Memory of Newton. Summer published; a second edition the same year. Thomson now relying on literature for his support. Britannia written (not published till 1729), in opposition to the peace-at-any-price policy of Walpole. The poet spends part of the summer at Marlborough Castle (the guest of the Countess of Hertford).

1728. Spring published by Andrew Millar. Goldsmith born.

1729. Death of Congreve: anonymous poem To the Memory of Congreve published; attributed to Thomson on very unsatisfactory evidence. In September, Thomson the guest of Bubb Dodington at Eastbury. The poet busy in various ways—with the tragedy of Sophonisba, the completion of The Seasons, the publication of Britannia, and contributions to Ralph's, Miscellany; among the last a Hymn, on Solitude, The Happy Man, and a metrical version of a passage of St. Matthew's Gospel.

1730. Publication of the first collected edition of The Seasons (including Autumn and the Hymn for the first time): two editions, one in quarto at a guinea, published by subscription; the other in octavo. Sophonisba produced at Drury Lane, February 28th, Mrs. Oldfield taking the part of the heroine: a success on the stage, despite one weak line, and selling well when printed. Travelling tutor to young Charles Talbot, son of Mr. Charles Talbot, then Solicitor-General (soon afterwards Lord Chancellor); in Paris in December, where (probably) he visits Voltaire.

1731. Visits most of the courts and capital cities of Europe (Murdoch); in Paris in October. Visits Italy—'I long to see the fields where Virgil gathered his immortal honey,' &c. Collecting material for his poem on Liberty. Correspondence with Dodington—' Should you inquire after my muse, I believe she did not cross the Channel with me.' Probably wrote, however, the lines on the death of Aikman, the painter. Returns to England in December. Birth of Cowper. The Gentleman's Magazine established.

1733. Death of young Talbot in September; the elder becomes Lord Chancellor in November; soon after, Thomson appointed Secretary of Briefs in the Court of Chancery—the post a sinecure with about 300l. a year. Some personal stanzas of The Castle of Indolence written about this time.

1735. Publication of Liberty; Parts I, II, and III, at intervals.

1736. Liberty, Parts IV and V at intervals. Thomson goes to live in Kew Lane, Richmond—his residence for the rest of his life. Intimacy with Pope, whose house was only a mile off, at Twickenham. Busy with the drama—'whipping and spurring to finish a tragedy this winter.' Sends pecuniary assistance to his sisters in Edinburgh. Becomes acquainted with 'Amanda'.

1737. Death of Lord Chancellor Talbot, in February; Thomson's memorial verses (panegyric and elegy) in June. Writing Agamemnon. Loss of Secretaryship. Acquaintance with George Lyttelton. Pension of 100l. a year from the Prince of Wales, to whom Liberty had been dedicated. Shenstone's Schoolmistress published.

1738. Thomson's Preface to Milton's Areopagitica appears. Agamemnon produced in April, Quin in the title role. A new edition (a reprint of octavo edition of 1730) of The Seasons brought out.

1739. Thomson's tragedy of Edward and Eleonora prohibited by the censorship.

1740. Conjointly with Malloch, The Masque of Alfred, containing the ode 'Rule, Britannia', performed August 1, in Clifden Gardens, before the Prince of Wales. 1742. Young's Night thoughts (Books I-III). 1743. Visits the Lytteltons, at Hagley Park, in August—'I am come to the most agreeable place and company in the world.' Correspondence with 'Amanda'.—' But wherever I am... I never cease to think of my loveliest Miss Young. You are part of my being; you mix with all my thoughts.' His song, For ever, Fortune, wilt thou prove, ' about this time. Preparing, at Hagley, a revised edition of The Seasons with Lyttelton's assistance.

1744. New edition of The Seasons, with many alterations and additions. Lyttelton in office: he appoints Thomson Surveyor-General of the Leeward Islands—a sinecure post, worth 300l. a year clear. Death of Pope.

1745. His best drama Tancred and Sigismunda produced at Drury Lane, with Garrick as Tancred. At Hagley in the summer.

1746. Thomson makes way for his friend (and deputy), William Paterson, in the office of Surveyor-General. At Hagley in the autumn. Last edition of The Seasons published in the poet's lifetime. Collins's Odes published.

1747. At Hagley in the autumn. Visits Shenstone at the Leasowes. Busy at Coriolanus (nearly finished in March).

1748. Prince of Wales's displeasure with Lyttelton visited on Lyttelton's friends—Thomson's name struck off pension list. The Castle of Indolence, in May. Death of Thomson, after short illness, at Richmond, August 27th. Buried in Richmond churchyard. Collins's Ode in memory of Thomson—a lasting memorial.

1749. Coriolanus produced, in January—the Prologue by Lyttelton.

1753. Shiels's Life of Thomson (Cibber's Life of the Poets)

1758. Death of Allan Ramsay.

1759. Birth of Burns.

1762. Murdoch's Memoir of Thomson (prefixed to an edition of Thomson's Works). Monument to Thomson in Westminster Abbey.

1781. Johnson's Life of Thomson (Lives of the Poets).

1791. Burns's Address to the Shade of Thomson.

1792. The Earl of Buchan's Essay on the Life of the Poet Thomson

1831. Biography of Thomson by Sir Harris Nicholas (prefixed to the Aldine Edition of Thomson's Works: annotated by P, Cunningham, 1860).

1842. An edition of The Seasons, with notes by Bolton Corney.

1891. Clarendon Press edition of The Seasons and The Castle of Indolence, with a biographical notice and full notes by J. Logie Robertson.

1894. Furth in Field (Part IV—On the poet of The Seasons), by Hugh Haliburton.

1895. James Thomson: Sa Vie et ses Oeuvres (678 pp.), by Leon Morel.

1898. James Thomson (in Famous Scots Series), by W. Bayne.

1908. James Thomson (in English Men of Letters Series), by G. C. Macaulay.

www.ingramcontent.com/pod-product-compliance
Lightning Source LLC
Chambersburg PA
CBHW022119040426
42450CB00006B/762